Antiquing Secrets

Fastest Way to Discover Antique History & Learn How to Collect Antiques Like a Seasoned Veteran

Bowe Packer

TABLE OF CONTENTS

PUBLISHERS NOTES

Disclaimer

This publication is intended to provide helpful and informative material. Please understand that this guide is intended to help get you off to a great start of learning about Antiques and is not the end all be all of antiques.

There is much to learn about this long living, vast hobby. You will run into things I did not, that is just the natural process of life. However, the author has made every effort to provide you with sound information at a good price.

The author and publisher specifically disclaim all responsibility for any liability, loss or risk, personal or otherwise, which is incurred as a consequence, directly or indirectly, from the use or application of any contents of this book.

Any and all product names referenced within this book are the trademarks of their respective owners. None of these owners have sponsored, authorized, endorsed, or approved this book.

Always read all information provided by the manufacturers' product labels before using their products. The author and publisher are not responsible for claims made by manufacturers.

Paperback Edition 2013

Manufactured in the United States of America

DEDICATION

I dedicate this book to all those people out there who remind us of the things we have forgotten about ourselves.

And this holds especially true of my beautiful and amazing wife, Alma. She is the one woman who has the most amazing talent to let me grow and love the things about myself that I have not fully accepted.

I cherish the love she has for me when I may not know how to love myself.

May we all have this kind of beautiful soul in our life.

Sent from LOVE,

Sunshine In My Soul

PART 1: PREPARING FOR THE ANTIQUE HUNT

So you think you want to collect antiques? Did you always have a passion for history? Or did you discover a unique item that is propelling you . . . nudging you . . . to go on the quest?

Either way, it's best before you start out to learn more about this amazingly complex, yet elegantly simple hobby. You are about to begin a journey that will entertain, educate, and excite you for the rest of your life. Guaranteed.

Introduction: Welcome To The Great Antique Hunt

For years, when friends would talk about their antique collections, I felt a little (okay, more than a little) intimidated. I used this standing joke when asked if I collected any artifacts, "Why of course! You should see the collection of dust I have at home. It's all over the house."

Since then, I've taken a second look at antiquing. I had always been a history buff, but then I found an actual historical item or two that I thought were really interesting, and that's all it took.

I was off. I had signed up, evidently, for the Great Antique Hunt. Unfortunately, I knew very little about the several pieces I initially purchased -- despite my knowledge of history. And my hunt was more like a game of pin the tail on the donkey. I felt blindfolded and as if someone had twirled me around. There I was making decisions upon which I knew very little. Needless to say, not all of them were the wisest.

In my first several months of collecting, I discovered -- looking back with that inevitable 20-20 hindsight -- how much money

I actually wasted on what I thought at the time were quality antique pieces

Finally, I was able to stop myself, take my blindfold off, and just digest the hobby a bit farther. And that made all a world of difference. The next several purchases I made not only delighted me, but were appraised and valued as a smart move. (Imagine that! Me! Performing some smart moves!)

And as I sat down one evening with a cup of tea, content in my day's purchases, I wondered how many others were wandering aimlessly like I had been. And that's when I vowed to write a small compendium that would give the novice antique collector a solid beginning in the hobby and provide the veteran with a great review.

Viola! The birth of a book

And yes, the result is this eBook, Creative Antiquing Secrets: What Every Antique Hunter Must Know. I've taken a close look at where my largest and most expensive mistakes were made and wrote about those topics. Of course, the purpose is to try to save you from the time and expense of making the same mistakes.

As you initially read through this book, you'll immediately see that it is divided into several subjects. Part I is entitled Preparing for the Antique Hunt. It encompasses the introduction and the first three chapters.

With the help of this book, you'll learn everything from exactly what constitutes an antique to how to negotiate in order to get the best price, as well as a chapter devoted solely to tips and techniques for getting the most for your money and the highest quality antiques you can find.

Part II, Pursuing Pottery deals specifically with the collection of pottery -- from England as well as America. And of course, we talk about pottery trends in history throughout Europe as well.

When it comes to identifying furniture, you'll want to turn to Part III. Again, the division of topics includes continental Europe, English and then American. In this section, you'll discover the joy that accompanies a find as well as the despair when you discover your piece isn't worth what you thought.

In the fourth section of this book, you'll discover what makes antique glassware . . . . well, antique. It's called Grabbing

Glassware. You'll also discover the difficulty involved in distinguishing glassware from continental Europe, England and America!

And finally, I've provided you with an appendix of resources to help you pursue your Great Antique Hunt, including the names of some very good organizations as well as a short glossary to help familiarize yourself with the terms you're guaranteed to hear on your journeys.

Ready to start this new adventure?

CHAPTER 1- IS IN THE EYE OF THE BEHOLDER

Tell me, exactly how do you spot that antique in the field? Some individuals -- usually those who know the least about antiques -- are quick to answer that. They readily spout off that an antique is any object that is at least 100 years old.

And to a certain degree, these folks are absolutely right. They just don't go quite far enough in their definition. Just because an object happens to be old, doesn't automatically make it an antique. Well, it doesn't make it a valuable antique -- one you would desire to own.

The antique "connoisseurs" argue that age alone can't define value. You must also look a little farther, especially toward the quality of an object, whether it is furniture, glassware or pottery. As one expert told me recently, "An item that was ugly and lacking in quality more than 100 years ago, is probably still ugly and of poor quality today."

Well said.

What about that "genuine reproduction"?

Sooner or later, even the most careful of antique hunters discover this. And they mutter choice words upon finding it out. Have you ever seen any furniture or other objects marked as "a genuine reproduction"? Friends of mine chuckle when they see this, immediately translating it into one word, "fake".

Well, consider this fact. Especially in the realm of furniture, those "genuine reproductions" themselves are now coming upon their 100th birthday. What would that make them? Well, yes, old. But technically, now we have genuine reproductions that are actually antiques. Does it make them collectibles as well? An excellent question. One, by the way, with no definitive answer.

The four-part antique litmus test

Generally speaking, when an antiques expert examines an object, he scrutinizes it in regard to four different areas. These four are not only legitimate categories, but really, if you think about it, are very practical as well: **Quality, condition, rarity and demand.**

True, trying to define quality in any quantifying way is a little difficult. Nonetheless it's one of the most important, and some would say the most important, aspects of analyzing the value of any antique. That's because quality is often viewed as "a level of excellence".

This means excellence not only in the conception of the piece being reviewed, but also in the design, and finally, in the execution, or the production, of the final product.

A cabinet that is well crafted is readily recognizable simply by its stability and how well it performs the function for which it was made. You will know it immediately. The doors open with ease, shut tightly and any drawers pull in and back out smoothly.

Not only that, but the finish on this cabinet is clean and the color is still vibrant. And the intricacies that make it an example of great carpentry are still in place.

In large part, the quality of an object simply implies that those who crafted this object paid close attention to all the details. In fact, you can go one step farther in the definition of quality. It implies that it was made with a certain level of "caring" and not just slapped together.

What is the condition of the object?

Too many people confuse these two elements. An antique may have been built with high quality materials, but in the 100 years since, its been abused in some way. Even though it began its life as a quality piece, the condition of this object may be less than excellent now.

It's obvious that a high quality antique in poor condition will undoubtedly fetch less in an antique shop or auction than the same high quality antique in excellent condition.

But now we come to an interesting angle regarding quality versus condition. The condition of an object often can be improved if you find the right professional who is very good at his work.

Quality, however, is a fixed trait. Nothing improves the quality of a poorly made piece of furniture. And that's exactly why an item deemed of poor quality will never be as valuable as an object that is of higher quality.

How many of these did you say were made? Rarity

Now that I've muddied the waters for you by combining quality and condition, I'm ready to add a little more sludge to the liquid. This would be in the form of what dealers like to call rarity.

Many people tend to confuse this with age. And you can easily see why. As the age of the object increases, it also increases the likelihood that fewer of them survive throughout the years. But this isn't always necessarily the case.

I always like to point individuals to the example of coins from the Early Roman Empire. These objects are nothing if not literally thousands of years old. Yet, few historians -- and fewer antique collectors -- consider them "rare".

Why? Because of the vast numbers of coins that were originally minted (probably in the thousands) as well as the high number of them that have survived and surfaced through archeological excavations and other means.

Would it surprise you to know that the vast majority of Roman coins are only worth the metal they contain? It's true!

Let's try looking at another example -- this one a little bit closer to our time period. It's been called the most famous style chair of the 19th century -- the Hitchcock chair. (And, no, it's not named after the film director Alfred Hitchcock!)

The chair was the brainchild and creation of furniture maker Lambert Hitchcock. Not only was it a great idea, but it ended up becoming an excellent and wildly popular chair. (You can see where I'm going with this already!)

In fact, thousands upon thousands of these so-called Hitchcock chairs were made. Production began in 1826 on -- believe it or not -- an assembly line in his factory in Connecticut.

Thousands of these mass-produced chairs can still be found today. They certainly qualify as antiques according to the age category. They are more than 180 years old. But, no antique dealer would dare call them rare. So, they are not likely to command a very high price at an auction or antique shop.

What if no one wants the darned thing? Demand

An excellent question. I have a friend who used to chuckle when someone pronounced the worth of his latest antique "find". "It's only worth that," he would laugh, "if someone is willing to pay that price."

While his approach was tongue-in-cheek, his comment was spot on. If there is no demand for a rare item of high quality in great condition, then it's likely that the item is not worth (at least at the moment) much at all.

Of course that doesn't mean it can't hold some value beyond cash to you. Perhaps it was Aunt Bertha's chair and Aunt Bertha was your favorite aunt. Well, then no amount of money, presumably, that would make you part with it.

What constitutes "demand?"

What, you wonder, dictates demand for an object? No single answer can adequately explain it. Several reasons may go into that explanation. First, it may be that the current state of the economy is poor. People just don't have the disposable income to spend on an item.

It may also be that some segment of the population doesn't appreciate its value and therefore has no interest in it. Or for one reason or another, it might be that a social or political stigma is now associated with the product.

Will this antique lose its current value?

"Will my antiques drop in value?" It's a question that is uppermost in most novice antique collectors and usually on the tip of their tongues. Many individuals are fearful of asking - some because they just don't want to hear the "wrong" answer.

I have a friend who is an antique dealer who loves to answer the question this way. "Your antiques will only drop in value if you break them."

Again, while humorous, this is close to the truth. Of course, no one can predict with any certainty the future prices of antiques. The best answer even the most knowledgeable expert can give is a waffling "Probably not".

For the most part, antiques hold their monetary value extremely well. There are instances when the value of a piece may take a nose dive. But these cases are rare and usually only temporary.

Of course, we hope you don't check the value of your antiques as regularly as day traders on the stock exchange. But if you have checked them out lately only to discover they've lost a little value, don't panic. Be patient. The drop is more than likely just a temporary one.

The exception to the rule: Introducing the "genuine reproduction"

Having said all of that, I must add just one small caveat here. There is one situation in which your antiques may fall in worth. That would be the introduction of reproductions into the marketplace.

But they have to be excellent reproductions. If an object can be reproduced so that it is indistinguishable from the original, then your original may, indeed, lose its value.

This, though, is a rare circumstance. It doesn't affect the value of antiques as much as it does newer collectibles, either.

For one thing, most reproductions have some trait about them that shouts out "reproduction". You may not be able to find it. Uncle Fred may not be able to find it. But an expert in that area of antiques will.

Your best defense against this is knowledge (go figure!). Read up on everything dealing with antiques -- magazines, books, information online. All of these sources will warn you if there are reproductions on the market that threaten the value of your collection.

How much did you pay for that thing, anyway?

The only sure way of losing money on your antique purchase is by paying too much for it in the first place. (Uh-oh! I see panic on your face!)

Here is a second example, though, of how keeping abreast of the news in the antique-collecting field can be extremely handy. Had you done your homework to begin with, you may not have bought the DigitWidget at that price. If you had consulted with websites or with any current books, you may have been able to discover this.

That's why it's so vital to maintain some links, -- either digitally or through books and magazine -- to the antiquing community at large. Such interaction on your part helps keep you aware of current prices.

Provenance: Does your antique purchase come with it?

Provenance. No it's not a city in Rhode Island. It's actually what antique experts call any information connected to the past of a certain object.

Provenance. Keep this word in mind. Believe it or not, it can actually add quite a bit of value to your antique. This is especially true if the information about it is extremely interesting or if it is connected to someone famous.

And if neither of those is true about the provenance of your antique, don't worry. Sometimes just your normal, run-of-the-mill back-story on an antique can increase its worth. You'd be surprised.

Let's say you have a Victorian settee. You know for a fact that it was owned, prior to you, by Sarah Pearl who lived down the road. In fact, you also know, for a fact, that Miss Pearl used this settee when she tutored students. There you have it, the provenance to your antique.

It may not sound like much of a story to you, but even that little bit of knowledge about that piece may help to increase its value. The bottom line is this: the more information available about a specific antique, the more desirable it is.

Antiques are your connection to history

Why? Well, part of the lure of antiquing is the relationship we feel with the past. When we -- you, me, and just about every other collector -- can then transform an abstract thought into a solid bond to something in the past, then it makes collecting all the more satisfying.

In some cases, you may actually have papers or receipts that back up and prove your provenance. If so, keep these under lock and key. This is especially true if the back-story of your antique talks about a famous person. If you can prove that George Washington slept on it or Abraham Lincoln bought it, then you can see why it would be an obvious advantage.

Now that you know a little about what distinguishes an antique from just an old object, let's help you learn your way around an antique shop, the local flea market, and your regional antique mall. Discover the fine art of negotiating the right price in the next chapter.

CHAPTER 2- WHAT IF THE PRICE ISN'T RIGHT? BARGAINING YOUR WAY TO A BETTER DEAL

I see you're reading up on the prices of antiques in that price guide. You do realize that the book is called a "guide" and not a price "bible"? That's because the prices in that book aren't written in stone. They can always be negotiated.

And even more than that, you may be able to find bargains just by being in the right place at the right time. It's true you know!

It's one of those secrets of antiquing that some professional collectors and many extreme amateur collectors might never tell you.

But it's a very valuable lesson. I would hate for you to learn it the hard way. Before you go antiquing next weekend, be sure that you've clued yourself in to the following hints. Keep in mind that "bargain shopping for antiques" is not an oxymoron.

Rule Number 1 of Antiquing: Shop Around, Shop Around

You've been busy reading those price guides and know what the going price for, let's say, a pie safe is. Well, you've seen several that are well within that range. Let's also say, for the sake of this example that you've already located two along the way in your shopping excursion. These are marked from $550 to $750. Just a little lower than what the guide tells you is the "going rate".

So, should you jump at them because you really want them added to your antique collection?

I say hold off. And I'll tell you why. Follow me into the next town over. Now we'll go into this small antique shop. Look at the price of Joe's pie safe. Yep. It was $500, but now, it's reduced to $450. Now, that's a bargain. I think this is the one you should purchase, don't you?

Why did he mark it down? No, there's not a thing wrong with it. It's just that Joe is, well, tired of staring at the thing day after day. He paid even less for it, and quite frankly, would like to get something out of his investment. His desire to move his inventory works in your favor.

But, had you bought the first or second pie safe you found, you wouldn't have experienced the joy of such a bargain. In fact, you might have walked in -- a previous pie safe purchase completed -- and tried to kick yourself in the . . . well, you know where.

It always pays to shop around. When looking for antiques, you need to have a certain attitude of "kismet" in your spirit. If you trounce through your shopping too rigidly aligned to discovering certain objects at specifically set prices, it could be deadly. Not only for your wallet, but for the joy of the chase as well.

I have to believe that whatever philosopher who said the joy was in the journey and not necessarily the destination was an antique hunter!

Rule Number 2 of Antiquing: Give Yourself a Maximum Limit

Antiquing can be like gambling in one very real sense -- it can be addictive. I have a friend who goes gambling with a set spending limit in hand. If he doesn't win after his initial maximum outlay is gone for that day, he is done.

And that's exactly what you might want to do with your spending limit on antiques. How much is the highest you're willing to spend for a specific item? This way, you won't be swept away by the moment. You're not caught up in the excitement of an auction or being talked into a higher price by some persuasive owner of an antique shop. Don't allow the pressure to make you spend more than you have set aside for that specific piece.

Rule Number 3 of Antiquing: Be Patient

And why not? It's an antique for crying out loud. It's only going to get better with age. It's not like it's a new item and you have to be the first on your block to get a new electronic toy.

If the antique has already been around for at least 100 years, what's another couple of months in the overall scheme of things?

And here's the first thing you're going to notice when you start seriously antiquing. There are far more antiques that anyone can seriously afford to own. I know you're excited about your new hobby, but you may very well buy yourself into the poor house if you don't use a little patience and pace yourself.

Buy only when you consider the price is right. Normally, I won't buy at all unless the piece I'm looking at is priced under the established price. Using patience and this method, I've been able to add quite a few valuable items to my collection. Of course it has taken me a while. But then again, I love the journey!

Rule Number 4 of Antiquing: Splurge on yourself once in a while

No, this really doesn't go against Rule #2 -- setting a maximum price. What this advice means is that once every so often, it does you good to indulge in an antique you thought you could only dream about.

That doesn't mean you spend more than what it's worth. Still, try to get it at the most inexpensive price you can. But if you can see that it's below market value and it's something you've been eyeing for a long, long time. . .well, you're definitely worth the splurge now, aren't you?

Rule Number 5 of Antiquing: Check out the "layaway" plan

Seriously. Many antique dealers and even more antique malls have layaway plans these days. Really want an item, but it's out of your price range? As long as it satisfies the other rules, -- you're still paying under market value for it, you're getting a good deal, that is you can't find it any cheaper anywhere else -- then go for it.

You'll discover that buying an antique this way is relatively painless, and for the most part, interest free. Most dealers and mall owners won't charge anything for this service. They're just happy to see that the piece is going to someone who appreciates it

Where are you looking?

The answer to this question can be as important as, if not more important, than what antique you're looking for. It seems such a natural thing to do. You consider yourself an antique collector (and indeed you are), so you haunt the antique stores and malls.

But did you ever wonder where some of their merchandise came from? Think garage sales, flea markets, and estate sales. Yes. And if you decide to expand the perimeters of your search, you may be able to grab some of those bargains.

Believe it or not, there is a strategy to shopping at a garage sale. The word is browse. I'm serious. I don't know what your collection looks like, but I try to keep mine open ended. I don't specialize in just furniture or glassware. I like to have an occasional piece that really doesn't fit into any current category I have.

And if you do this, you may be able to get some really good bargains. Several months ago I was at a yard sale. I was looking for books that day. This particular garage sale had no books. But I spotted this lamp. I could have sworn I saw one identical to it on The Antiques Road Show. And it was only a couple of dollars. So I decided to purchase it. Sure enough, it was worth at least ten times what I paid for it.

But I never would have discovered such a serendipitous find if I refused to look at anything else but books!

There's a method to your madness: Shopping the garage sales!

Believe it or not, there's a certain technique to shopping garage sales and flea markets. Those of us who have done this for long nearly take it for granted. We just assume that everyone knows the hidden secrets to getting a bargain. But the more I talk to people, the more I realize that many just don't know these "secrets".

First, you need to walk a tightrope. While you have certain ideas of what you want, you need to be open minded enough to look around at everything. You just never know where the next bargain is buried.

With that in mind, I always start my garage sale hunting on Saturdays by making a list. But I am always willing to look for items not on my list as well.

How to find garage sales

The next secret is finding the garage sales themselves. You could drive aimlessly around town for hours searching for them, but why? Why not just pick up a local paper? Most newspapers have a listing of local garage sales in the classified section

I start the day before -- after all, most people host weekend events -- and make notes of the ones that sound the best. Then I find out where they are located. I visit these based on geography. I try to get the most bang for my gas tank buck! And now with the GPS technology in cell phones, this has become easier than ever!

Another tip on the location of the garage sale: the more upscale the neighborhood, the more likely it is you'll find quality items. While you may find some tucked away along the poor side of town, chances are slim that this will occur.

When to hit the garage sales? Timing is everything!

Timing your visit to garage sales is important too! If you go early, you'll find the best selections, of course. (Some flea market dealers try to get to the sales even before their printed opening times!) But if you go late, you find some of the best bargains.

One of the habits I've developed is to leave the home owner my cell phone number if I find a great item in the morning, but don't want to pay the price. If it doesn't sell, I ask her to call me if she wants to sell it at the end of the day at a lower price. I've gotten some great bargains this way. It's risky though. If you really, really want the item, you may be better off just to buy it outright in the morning!

Sometimes you can purchase the item at a reduced price just by saying to the host "But all I have with me is $10." Depending on how badly the person wants to sell the item, what time of day it is, and what the item is, this technique works. But for heaven's sake, don't say you only have $10 and then casually toss out a $20! You can undermine your efforts fast!

Now, you're almost armed with all the practical knowledge you can possibly use for getting the best bargains for your collection. But not quite. The next chapter contains a few more tips . . . techniques . . . and tricks to help you build a great collection without driving yourself into the poorhouse!

CHAPTER 3- TIPS, TRICKS, & TECHNIQUES EVERY ANTIQUE HUNTER SHOULD KNOW

Yes, I agree that piece looks like it's in excellent condition. No, I have no way to determine that for sure. I'm just giving it a good examination with my naked eye. Wait! What do you have there? Planning on dancing in this antique shop?

Are you telling me that black light you have can actually date that object and see if some small piece of it has been repaired? All in one fell swoop? Wow! I've got to get one of those. Please, by all means, show and tell me more!

Let's face it. Some crucial clues that can lead you to the age of an object or those very small telltale signs that are vital in detecting possible past repairs can be critical when you're purchasing an antique.

Laugh if you like at the black light method. Once you see it in action, my guess is that you'll laugh no more. The idea is really quite simple. Some images that you just won't be able to see in our normal range of spectrum light, become glaring faults when placed under an ultraviolet light.

Don't get the wrong idea. Using a black light on an object is not the ultimate test for it. In fact, in many ways, it's just the beginning. Here are six very good methods of making use of black light when checking out antiques.

1. Detecting Repairs on Porcelain.

It's true! You really should be making the black light test a standard habit if you're a serious porcelain collector. Simply take the piece you're interested in into a dark room. You can use either the larger handheld black light or the smaller variety which fits on your keychain.

If the repair to the porcelain is of excellent quality, then chances are good you're not going to notice it using just your eye. You'll need a little help. Shine that black light onto that repaired piece and you'll realize what I mean when I say the repair becomes "obvious".

Not only that, but the newer, modern paints glow under black light. You can see, then, that this is another great way about verifying its past.

2. The Reproduction Glass Test

If you have green Depression glass or Vaseline glass, place a black light under these. You'll notice that they glow. They glow due to the quantity of uranium oxide in the glass itself. American colorless pressed glass, which was made prior to 1930, glows yellow. Reproductions of any the those three don't glow at all.

American brilliant cut glass, according to some antique experts, glows with a yellow hue when placed under an ultraviolet light. Other experts swear it casts a pale violet or even blue tint. Before you rely on a black light for any of these, you should dig a bit deeper to find out for sure if the color the glass should glow.

3. Artwork and the Black Light

But the connection isn't what you might think! Modern paint fluoresces under a black light -- as we've already mentioned with regard to porcelain. This instrument, then, is the perfect tool to detect any later day touch ups on the artwork.

You can also use this to discover any possible hairline cracks in oil paintings. They become much more visible in this spectrum of light.

If you're thinking about becoming a collector of fine art -- or are already starting a small collection -- you may want to invest in a book that gives you more detail on reading the results of the black light. It may be able to save you from making a dreadful error of judgment.

4. Photos, Postcards, and Paper Products

Okay, here is my area of weakness: old photos -- of anyone's family, as well as old postcards. I love to buy them sometimes just to buy them. But now, I can tell their age a little more precisely. Paper products made prior to the 1930s rarely, if ever, glow under this instrument.

Paper products created after the 1930s will glow. This is because of the various chemical bleaches and dyes used in the papermaking process after those years.

This piece of information also helps in detecting forged documents as well. You can also distinguish reproductions with the black light in just about all types of ephemera. Just a word of caution here: if you're thinking about buying any piece of rare paper memorabilia, get it appraised by a professional. He'll not only have a better set of tools with which to determine its authenticity, he'll also be carrying around a wealth of knowledge about the subject that you may not have.

5. Verifying Age of Cast Iron

Yes, indeed. The black light can also be used to authenticate the age of cast iron, whether it's been molded into a bank, mechanical toy, a doorstop, or any other piece from the early 1900s. The articles with the original paint are valuable, but knowing if the piece you're holding is one with original paint has been, for the longest time, difficult.

If it glows, then you know that a modern paint has been used, to perhaps brush the item up, which only brings its value down. If the paint doesn't glow when you turn on the black light, then you can look elsewhere on the article for its authenticity.

Tools of the Trade

Indeed, if you're on the Great Antique Hunt, you can't leave home without the proper tools. Below are just several tools that you should buy yourself even before you make your first antique purchase.

Buy a magnifying glass or a jeweler's loupe -- or why not both? Why not, indeed! These items are every antique hunter's stock in trade. You'll discover you will end up using them to help you read small marks and signatures on all sorts of porcelain or pottery pieces.

Both of these items are perfectly suited to help you examine any type of damage on the articles you're interested in. You can even use these to distinguish between hand-painted techniques and decals and transfers.

Yes, both of these tools can come in amazingly handy. Think about keeping at least one of them -- perhaps the jeweler's loupe -- at your desk and another in your purse somewhere while you drive. You'll also discover that many of these come in extraordinarily handy, especially if you chose the type with their own case.

Get yourself a decent digital camera. This is where high-tech meets old- fashioned, Old World objects. Why do you need a camera? The ability to photograph your collection is in itself priceless. Let's hope your collectibles are never stolen, but if they are, you have photos to show your insurance company. You also have photos ready if you ever want to see a piece or two.

Don't think you have to invest in some expensive camera either. You are looking for one with macro features for capturing details and for small objects. There are plenty of resources to help you choose the one that suits your purposes.

Along these same lines, think about getting what many antique hunters call affectionately, "a photo studio in a box". The name just about sums the product up at that.

As part of your efforts at documenting your collection, you'll want the photos you take to be the highest quality possible. Sometimes natural lighting or indoor lamp lighting just isn't good enough. This unique invention supplies you with everything you need in one, easy-to-use kit. Check it out!

Now, we're ready to dig into the real meat of antique collecting: learning about some of the possibilities of what to collect. The following, I'm sure you'll realize, is only a small snippet of what's available. It is, however, among the most popular collections. And that's exactly why they're included in this book. Let's dig in!

PART 2: PURSUING POTTERY

You have to believe that when ancient man finally created pottery, cave moms across the world were united in saying, "You need to eat everything on that plate!"

And it also makes you wonder how those cave families then decided who would wash the pottery after meals. It could have the start of a whole new set of disagreements.

For the antique collector, pottery poses a different set of questions. In fact it's quite a puzzling piece for those who yearn to hunt and collect this type of artifact. You're about to discover just how puzzling pottery can be.

CHAPTER 4- PIECING TOGETHER THE GREAT ENGLISH POTTERY PUZZLE

In our modern day, we're all used to entering a department store, going to the kitchen section, and admiring the pottery. Curious about who made it? Flip it over and the underside gives you the manufacture's name. It's as simple as that.

Try that with a piece from the 17th, 18th, or even the 19th centuries. More often than not, you're going to discover the bottom is void of any name. Many times these pieces were made by craftsman referred to as studio potters. And they never thought to sign or identify their pieces. The work they were performing, as far as they were concerned, was more about practical matters.

Of course, there is some definite identification to be made. Quite frankly, piecing together the pottery puzzle is one of the primary joys of the hobby.

Among the most important creations of English pottery is London-based Metropolitan Ware, as well as the centers of Wrotham, Kent and Staffordshire. Some of the most influential names in pottery are rooted in these four cities, including Toft, Simpson and Malkin.

English pottery can be identified additionally through a technique called graffito. It's a form of decorating the pottery with a coating of a light color to a dark body. This practice was used extensively in the English are of Devonshire.

Astbury & Whieldon Of Staffordshire

While certainly there were many potters in the mid-18th century, two of them are particularly interesting to the antique collector. Both hail from Staffordshire. Just the sheer size of the size of their output was amazing. They are Whieldon and Astbury.

The Enchanting Toby Jug

Whieldon's name, in fact, is nearly synonymous with pieces that possess a pale-colored transparent glaze. He also created early versions of the Toby jug.

A Toby jug? Yes! Have you ever heard of them? Ah, if you haven't, you're in for a rare treat. Sometimes referred to as a Filpot or Philpot, this is a pottery jug that is created in the form of a seated person (believe it or not!). Sometimes, the jug is in the shape of the head of a recognizable person. Very often, in England, that meant the shape of a king.

In many instances the figure is appears jovial. He holds a mug of beer in one hand and a pipe in the other. Additionally, he wears the typical 18th century tri-cornered hat, which is conveniently used as the pouring spout. Many times these jugs have lids with them as well as a handle attached in the rear!

If you're interested in collecting these, by the way, you may want to speak with football star Peyton Manning. It's said that he has the largest collection of Toby jugs in North America.

If you don't find Whieldon's original pieces, you may be able to find pottery resembling his made by a father and son team: Ralph Wood, Senior and Junior.

Astbury is noted for working with both red clay and white. With the aid of an engine turned lathe, many of his best pieces are of white clay decorated in relief.

Both Astbury and Whieldon, by the way, created lead-glazed pottery.

Meet Josiah Wedgwood: His reputation precedes him

While Astbury and Whieldon were excellent at this form, it was really the domain of a man named Josiah Wedgwood. You've probably heard of that name. A practical potter, Wedgwood actually became a much better businessman than potter (and he was a darned good potter!). His signature cream-colored, lead-glazed earthenware, was referred to from 1765 on as simply "queenware".

It was so prized, that many considered it to be every bit the quality of fine porcelain. Wedgwood's employees in Staffordshire decorated most of these items at a workshop located in London.

But a portion of this work was also performed in Liverpool to be decorated using a newly-developed process. This process involved using engravings that had been printed on paper, then transferred to the pottery itself.

At the beginning of the 19th century, luster-decorated pieces began to emerge. These were either decorated in silver or copper. This advancement in pottery making began to be used on all kinds of pieces.

The rarest find to date is a silver luster piece on a canary-yellow ground. Another widely sought after antique form of luster is the silver with an underlying of blue. And if the blue is in the shape of an object, then it's extremely rare. If you find this, you've pulled off an antique coup.

Let's talk white-glazed pottery

And why not? Originally developed to compete with the porcelain of the 1780s, white-glazed pottery became the favorite variety of many potters. Because of this, it was produced in great quantities. You can tell the early pieces from the later ones without too much trouble if you know what you're looking for.

The first pieces created possess decorations printed only in an under glaze of blue. By contrast, the later pieces appeared in a range of different colors. Enough pieces were made to create complete services.

Another important innovation belongs to the 19th century. This is ironstone china, so named -- at least this is what the legend says -- because it originally contained ironstone slag. If nothing else, the pieces were strong . . . so strong, in fact, they were nearly unbreakable. Just how durable was this ironstone? Some pieces are still in actual use today! Now that's durability.

Other traits that made this the pottery of choice in many homes were its reasonable price and its beauty. Found in vivid blues and reds, ironstone china carried decorations reminiscent of the orient.

Welcome to the world of stoneware

That brings us to stoneware. Non-porous, stoneware is a very hard variety of pottery. It wasn't a native development of England. Rather it came to the island via Germany. Curiously, stoneware differed from the other styles of pottery with the addition of salt to the kiln. If you ever hear someone refer to salt-glazed stoneware this is what they are talking about.

The addition of the salt, though it may seem a bit puzzling, was actually an act of genius. It proved to give the stoneware much more versatility. Not only was it hard and water-tight, but it was also capable of being made into much thinner pieces than other pottery.

Nottingham: More than just Robin Hood

Of course you've heard of Nottingham. It's the home of the legendary Robin Hood and his merry men. But now you can associate this area with the growth of stoneware as well.

In fact, it was the center of the stoneware world starting in the late 17th century. You'll recognize many of the pieces from

Nottingham by their hard grey body and the brown glaze with the texture much like -- believe it or not -- an orange peel. Derbyshire also developed into a center for the creation of stoneware.

Meanwhile . . . Back In Staffordshire

Two Dutch brothers, Elers, created a red stoneware which imitated some of the pieces being imported from China at the time. Originally, these two had worked with a potter name John Dwight at Fulham.

Originally, Dwight created stoneware that was grayish, but eventually he refined it until it was nearly white. Shortly after this perfection, the salt-glazed pottery was being manufactured across all of Staffordshire. Not surprisingly, the manufacture of this amazing pottery spread to Liverpool and several other areas.

Not only were plates, bowls and other kitchen necessities made from stoneware, but because it was able to be made so thin, figurines could also be created. Many of these had raised patterns. And the very thin layer of glaze didn't clog the small delicate lines of the objects.

Jasperware, anyone?

Eventually pottery fell to the growing demand for and popularity of porcelain. That didn't deter Wedgwood however. If you recall, we said he was not only a good potter, but a shrewd businessman as well. And here is where he shines.

In response, he quickly refined his pottery even further, developing another innovative style, this one known as jasperware. You can find literally thousands of relief portraits in this style, as well as plaques and vases.

The most common color of jasper ware is blue -- and this is good to know as a collector. But you can also find it in many light shades of yellow, green and lilac.

Additionally, Wedgwood created a black stoneware (he was, indeed, a busy man!), known as basalts, red stoneware called rosso antico and buff-colored stoneware, labeled cane ware.

The amazing thing is that Wedgwood's ancestors have never stopped making jasperware since the 18th century. You can still buy contemporary pieces today!

One other type of stoneware, brown, was also created throughout the 19th century. If you encounter any of this, though, you'll discover that the quality is not nearly as good as the other styles.

Thank you continental potters: Tin-glazed earthen ware

Indeed innovations in pottery making came about with the help of the potters of the European continent. They used an opaque white-glazed on which they painted designs of various colors. Originating in Italy, this pottery was finished with a glaze that contained an oxide of tin.

Tin was plentiful in England so it just seemed a natural addition to the repertoire of the English-based potter. It became known as delft ware after the similar work being produced in Delft, Holland.

When you first start collecting, you may have difficulty telling the difference from those that were produced in England and those produced in Holland.

This really isn't very surprising, considering it was the Dutch immigrants who brought this particular style to the Island.

Collecting pottery - can be more than a little confounding

As a novice antique collector, you're liable to be more than a little confused right about now -- if not just a bit intimidated. Given that, I hate to provide you with any more facts that may rattle your senses, but this is too important to ignore. Please bear with me a moment longer.

Pottery was made in England by native Dutch settlers who clearly copied Chinese originals (can you see how this can get confusing already?). These same objects were being copied by Dutch potters living in Holland as well (and the plot thickens!).

The English-crafted pieces are unmarked. (Now that figures, doesn't it?) This mans that only those 17th-century wares clearly marked can be ascribed to London craftsmen. Some of these, indeed, were wine bottles made from 1637 to 1672. These bottles also have the names of the type of wine on them as well.

If nothing else, collecting antique pottery forces you to learn quite a bit about English history as well as some European history. And as you go along you'll discover that uncovering interesting facts that go with this pottery is a large part of the collecting habit.

Now, are you ready to learn more about some continental European pottery? That's what the following chapter is all about!

CHAPTER 5- FINDING CLUES TO CONTINENTAL POTTERY

If you thought that the English pottery you've been looking at is a bit confusing, wait until you step foot on continental Europe! You'll need to be a virtual Miss Maple to piece together the clues in some cases on the origins and ages of the pottery there.

But then again, the thrill is in the hunt as they say. Searching for pottery from various countries in Europe is indeed a hunt worth taking.

You may not have known its name, but you immediately recognize the brilliant colors of pottery that originate from Spain. Indeed, they tend to be so distinctive that even those individuals who don't collect antiques or know much about pottery are still somehow able to recognize their unique appearance.

The Moorish conquerors of Spain, who had learned many pottery techniques from the Near Eastern craftsmen, established several potteries in Spain. The Moors used an earthenware that was decorated in a brilliant copper-colored luster. Known as Hispano-Moresque, the Spaniards continued this beautiful tradition even after the Moors withdrew from the country.

These pieces eventually found their way to Italy via an island called Majorca. It was mistakenly believed by many that the pottery actually originated on this island. For this reason, it understandably -- if mistakenly -- became known as majolica.

When you think majolica, you should think delftware of England. You nod politely, but I can see that "glaze" in your eyes. You're not sure why. And the answer really lies with several other countries that ended up creating great imitations of this beautiful pottery. One of these countries locations was Delft, Holland, which has a fine pottery reputation on its own.

Italy also became a center for the creation of majolica as did several other European centers. Once again, it's not as easy as it may seem to discern the origin, let alone the time period, of another style of pottery. The vast majority of these pieces were created between the 15th and 16th centuries. Yes, they were still being made later than that, but the quality of these later pieces cannot match the high quality of the earlier work. If you get serious about collecting, you'll see exactly what I mean.

Dutch tin-glazed

We covered delftware briefly in talking about English pottery, but its popularity also spread throughout Europe. Continuing to be made in Holland, much of the production was sent to England. Not only were dishes as well as other practical items sent, but so were decorative tiles.

Eventually tiles actually gained enough popularity that the creation of tiles grew to become a new branch of the pottery business. In fact, some craftsmen specialized only in the making of these tiles. It's not uncommon to find that an entire set of tile had been made so that when they are pieced together, a delightful depiction of a scene is formed.

German-made pottery

Don't overlook Germany when it comes to antique pottery. Potters from this country were also busy carefully and lovingly creating tin-glazed wares. Those of the highest quality came from cities like Hamburg, Frankfurt, Baireuth, Nanau and Nuremburg.

Much of the material produced resembles pottery being made at the same time in any number of other European countries. It's especially difficult to distinguish German pottery from that of England or Dutch during the same period.

If you're hunting lead-glazed pieces, you may be lucky enough to find German-made ones which were inscribed and dated. Many Germans, as well as Swiss professionals ensured that their work at least carried this much information especially if it were adorned with the graffito style.

German stoneware centers with reputations for quality included Cologne and Siegburg. The majority of these pieces were elaborately decorated. These two centers were also known for the creation of bellarmines, jugs with fat bodies and short thin necks. Additionally, these pieces also carried the depiction of a bearded man on the front. In this way, they may remind you of the English Toby jug.

Fraud? Did you say fraud?

Unfortunately, yes, fraud. Among many antique collectors there exists a belief that one class of pottery was extensively imitated purposely to be passed off as the real antique deal, even though it was nothing more than a "genuine reproduction".

In fact, Geoffrey Willis in his book "Practical Guide to Antique Collecting", describes this by saying "no class of pottery has been so widely copied for fraud."

So what is it? Sixteenth-century wares executed by Bernard Palissy, whose lifespan, by the way, covered most of that century. Among other pieces, he made dishes decorated with leaves, shells, fish, and even lizards.

You'll discover that these were placed on white clay effectively layered with a transparent glaze. Palissy, as you might guess, quickly garnered a following. There were those who imitated him because imitation is, after all, "the greatest form of flattery." And there were those who perfected his style purposely for fraudulent reasons.

Sixty pieces . . . And counting

If someone approaches you while you're on your quest for antiques explaining they have some genuine stoneware created at St. Porchaire, be wary. Extremely wary.

Currently, there are only 60 known pieces of this stoneware in existence. If someone is claiming to own a piece, the chances are far better that it's a "genuine reproduction" - that is a fake. If in doubt of any piece's authenticity, get it appraised by a professional.

The pottery from St. Porchaire is decorated in an unusual manner. The patterns were impressed using small metal stamps. The resulting marks were then filled with clays of different colors.

Ironically, its entire history has involved some source of contention among experts. Many believe that the center of manufacturing of this style was located in Lyons. Then it was thought to have been at Beauvais. Others contend that Orion is its original home.

Italian Influence

Many French potters were influenced by the work of Italians. Probably many more than we could ever realize. This influence, however, was short-lived. By the 17th century, the factory located at Rouen was making clearly Moorish-inspired tin-glazed majolica.

Even today, there's no doubt among collectors that French Faience rivals the finest porcelain pieces. Not only is it well-made and painted with care, but the shapes on the pieces are interesting and in many cases, unique.

And now it's time to talk about American-made pottery. Slow to come into its own, but still a delight to collect. You'll see exactly what I mean as we enter the next chapter!

CHAPTER 6- AMERICAN POTTERY - CAN YOU IDENTIFY THIS?

So you decided to collect native American-made pottery? You, indeed, then must truly love the thrill of the hunt. Anything collectible in this category is, quite frankly, quite scarce. Oh, but that's not to say the chase itself isn't thrilling and adventurous.

The scarcity of American pottery may surprise you. It startles many collectors -- me being one of them. After all, it's a known fact that some of the earliest inhabitants of North America were almost by second nature potters -- and they were very skilled and artistic.

By all logical reasoning, the New World should have been the perfect proving grounds for ambitious potters. When it came to natural resources, colonial America had it all -- in a very real sense.

American soil: Everything a potter could ask for!

Clay suitable for pottery was abundant. The common red-burning clays used for bricks roof tiles and coarse redware occurred naturally in shale or very close to the ground's surface.

The use of this type of clay only needed the very simplest of kilns and equipment. It would seem perfect for settlers in a new land.

Buff-burning clays were also available. There were of a finer texture and used since the 17th century. They usually were part of the more "experimental" pieces of just about every style.

By the 1800s, in fact, if you could look from above and see the composition and placement of pottery factories, you would see that they spread from Bennington to Baltimore and on westward along the Ohio River.

White-burning pipe clay: An American legacy

White-burning pipe clay had been used by the Native Americans even before the arrival of the colonists. The Europeans then began making them as well. The first known of these was in 1690 in Philadelphia.

It was long after -- 1720, to be precise – that these pipes were advertised by Richard Warder. Not only that, Andrew Duche discovered a vein in 1738 that seemed of "an earth" -- actually true kaolin, which is china clay. This ran from Virginia through the Carolinas and well into George. It could be seen because part of it was exposed along river banks in this area and along old stream beds.

Without a doubt, you can view examples of their craftsmanship in museums nationwide. But to actually purchase these for a private collection. . .that's another matter. You may find an opportunity, but it would be rare.

Early colonial pottery

You're in a similar dilemma when you search for early colonial pottery. In the mid-1640s, the few inhabitants who were settling along the coast no doubt made their own pottery. Surely it didn't take them long to either imitate the natives or to discover on their own the clay required for this activity.

But the setting in which they were placed was one of survival, not one of thriving. The pieces they made naturally reflected this. The pottery being created at this time in the new colonies reflected a purely utilitarian flavor. They were made out of necessity, not out of any artistic need.

Consequently, there was no need for anyone to sign their name to these pieces or even to hand them down from family member to family member. They were made, used, probably broken as a natural part of their being used, and then more pieces were made. The colonists' intent and needs were definitely not along the lines of artistic display

That's exactly how it stayed until about the first three-quarters of the 18th century. That's when you could feel a change in the air. Specifically, you need only look at the activities of the Crolius and Remney families at Potters' Hill, New York City. Or take a quick trip down to Burlington, New Jersey where Daniel Coxe was busy. He was creating what he labeled "White Chiney Ware".

All one has to do is peruse the newspapers of the time. They clearly show that pottery -- and even porcelain -- was being imported not only from England, but also from the Far East.

New England possessed no native stoneware clays. However, the shipping lanes at the time ensured that suppliers were found. Most notably used were potters from New Jersey and Stanton Island.

But while these may have been what the wealthier families wanted to display in their homes, it still left the vast majority of American-made wares little more than being of utilitarian bent.

It wasn't until 1730, in fact, that the first stoneware kiln was built by Clarkson Crolius in lower Manhattan. Also in that year, Anthony Duche of Philadelphia along with his sons petitioned the state assembly in support of "the Art of making stoneware." They had been working in the field, it seems, for several years.

Red-clay earthenware dated 1775: A rare find

It's no surprise then that not much made before 1800 in America even survives. You can literally point to single items, carefully encased in museums, as near miraculous examples of survival. In a museum in Brooklyn a bowl is on display. Made of Pennsylvania red earthenware, it's actually dated 1775. But this is the very rare exception.

The same Brooklyn-based museum also has a piece crafted in Philadelphia. Experts believe that it is actually a copy of a Liverpool-imported ware. It's decorated with a distinctly Chinese landscape in blue.

I like fine things Even when They are not mine, And cannot become mine; I still enjoy them.

- This translated from Pennsylvania dialect, appears on a sgraffiato plate signed by Johannes Leman, made before 1830 at the Friedrich Hildebrand pottery near Tyler's Port, Montgomery County, Pennsylvania.

Even though the east coast of America provided an abundance of both red and white clay, sometimes a potter wished to use another type of raw material. This proved to be of little problem for him, since riverboats were plentiful and could bring him just about anything.

So what did the first settlers make?

If you really think of it, this should come as no surprise. The early colonial pottery business was not built upon luxury decorative pieces. Nor surprisingly, were there huge orders for useful dinnerware pieces. Although they certainly existed.

No, the earliest demand was for brick-making. (Okay, so this isn't very exotic!) And this profession was recorded as far back as 1612 in Virginia. The cities of Boston and Salem record such businesses in 1629 and 1635.

Soon, you find such laws as the roof tiles or "tile art for House covering" appearing in the Massachusetts court orders. The first known instance of this was in 1646. By 1869, if you were a tile maker in Virginia, you were probably molding yourself out a good living.

In 1635, the potter, Philip Drinker came to Charlestown. This is the same year that "potbakers" William Vinson and John Pride were working in Salem.

The colonies were all abuzz in 1857 by the arrival of one truly extraordinary potter. His name was Dirck Claessen. In a short three years, he clearly established himself at Potbakers Corner in New Amsterdam -- now better known as New York City.

As the 18th century progressed, you began to see more pieces. Red clay was being used to craft baking dishes, for example. But these pieces imitate their English counterparts so closely you can't tell the difference. Even when the New World potters used the sgraffito decoration, they kept to the original German pattern so that it is actually indistinguishable from the European version.

American salt-glazed stone

Antique experts and historians alike have confirmed that American-made salt-glazed stoneware did exist. There is a tall round butter churn thought to be created about 1800 by Clarkson Crolius Senior. It's owned by the New York Historical Society.

At about the same time, it's known that pottery was set up for the creation of creamware. The purpose of this was to compete with the imported Wedgwood. Named Tivoli Ware, the firm advertised for orders as well as sought apprentices.

So what was the missing puzzle piece?

With all the talent and natural resources, you might expect to find more pieces from this era. But you look at your collection and you don't. And you look at your friend's collection and he doesn't. So what gives?

One essential puzzle piece appeared to be missing. And that was demand. There just wasn't a market for the pottery. The actual number of American colonists was actually quite small.

There were no more than 200,000 by 1690. Of that, the five largest towns on this side of the Atlantic only accounted for a scant 18,600 inhabitants.

Even taking into account that the population doubled every 20 years, by the year of independence, 1776, American society was still without a doubt a village-based country. This was true, despite the fact that the total population had now swarmed to 2,500,000. Philadelphia, with its 40,000 residents, was actually the second largest British City in the Empire (prior to the colonists declaring their freedom from England.).

Of all of these inhabitants, though, the vast majority -- some 90 percent -- lived in rural enclaves. The ensuing problem: there really was no growing demand for tradesmen like potters.

The early colonies: Clearly English in nature

Take, for example, the southern colonies. From Chesapeake society to the south, the English character of plantation life was clearly imprinted on society. Local commodities may have been exchanged for English luxuries, so there was no need to produce American-made pieces. The residents here viewed themselves as English and wanted English trends and English-made products.

Here again, though, is where a healthy dose of history helps keep your antique knowledge sharp. England, as you may or may not recall, actual suppressed colonial manufacturers at one point. In fact, General Thomas Gage, expressed the official British line in his letter to Lord Barrington in 1772. "It would be in the best economic interest of Britain to keep the settlers along the seacoast for as long as possible."

Additionally, English policy should be to "cramp their Trade as far as can be done prudentially." In many ways this statement was out of touch with what was really occurring in the colonies. Native manufacturing was indeed flourishing.

New England pottery shines!

All but the pottery trade, that is. Surprising, too, that it was New England that would discover the greatest success, which in the early years actually shipped raw materials to its craftsmen.

Indeed, it seems a most unlikely success story. But those are often the most pleasing. The main uses were in the kitchen or at the dinner table next to the pewter and woodenware. The pottery pieces were splashed with a pleasing color before being glazed with browns, yellows, and a variety of other rich and vibrant colors.

In order to obtain this effect, though, the least amount of equipment a potter could use was a horse-powered mill for the grinding and mixing of clay, as well as a homemade potter's wheel, a couple of wooden tools and maybe a couple of molds.

The potters who created these stunning pieces were seldom full-time tradesmen. More often than not they were what became known in the day as "bluebird" potters. These are individuals who worked when their other affairs permitted.

This same potter may be seen carrying his wares by wagon throughout the nearby communities. In some cases the "potshops" as they were called, might employ a certain amount of untrained young men or a migrant journeyman.

Got milk . . .Pans, that is?

Of course, even in this wilderness, American pottery holds a few surprises. And so it is with the case of an early -- and indeed curious -- milk pan said to be created by Andrew Duche.

The pan is said to have been discovered at a site near the Salzburger area 45- minutes from Savannah, GA. It's a heavy, thick and flat-footed article apparently made from area riverbank clays. Additionally, the body itself is textured and a mottled reddish brown.

The glaze of this piece is a clear straw-colored lead which is used over the entire glazed bottom flat of the pan with no rim or ridge.

The rise of communal society

Shortly after this, another southern pottery community established itself near a colony of Moravians in 1753. The pottery which had been in Bethlehem, Pennsylvania migrated to what was then the wilderness of Wachovia, North Carolina.

The religious group, United Brethren, founded a communal society with Brother Gottied Aust as potter. Firing his first kiln in the village of Bethabara in 1756, Aust made redware, pipes, stove tiles and a host of other pieces. He conducted public sales in 1761 which attracted the attention of individuals from a surprising distance away.

The entire enterprise eventually was transferred to the town of Salem, North Carolina in 1768. A mere six years later, in 1774, this firm was selling wares that far exceeded its capability in Salem. Production here lasted until roughly 1830.

Pennsylvania Dutch

No discussion of Early American pottery would be complete without the inclusion of a uniquely American group: the Pennsylvania Dutch. It's ironic that a group, so grounded in Old World ways and customs, can be viewed as a truly American legacy. But the truth is, -- group can!

The term refers to a blend of peoples from the Swiss Mennonites and Germans from the Palatinate, who settled in southeast Pennsylvania in the 18th century. The pottery of these people stand in marked contrast to the work created during the same time period in New England.

The Pennsylvania Dutch used color liberally, made of a wide range of various ideas and allowed their unique sense of humor to shine through their work.

The pieces that have survived the years reflect all of this -- and more. The flat Pennsylvania fruit pie dish, called a poischissel, was indeed an article not to be mistaken with anything made in New England. The pots for apple butter, known as epfel buther haffa, as well as the flowerpots known as bluma haffa were all distinctly unique.

Fluted turk's head cake molds were produced in a wide array of sizes and kinds. And this doesn't even begin to cover the quaint banks, bird whistles and double-walled tobacco jars which they made with an amazing precision.

The mighty Shenandoah Valley

If you travel just south of the state of Pennsylvania, you'll discover at about this same time, a group of potters (quite a few of them actually) which flourished throughout most of the 19th century. They were found in a region that stretched roughly 100 miles along the Shenandoah Valley.

Among the leaders of this group were members of the Bell family. The patriarch, Peter Bell, began making pottery beginning in 1800 and continued until 1845. He produced pieces in such various cities as Hagerstown, Maryland and Winchester, Virginia.

His eldest son, John Bell, continued in his father's footsteps working from 1833 until 1880 in Waynesboro, Pennsylvania. He was followed by five sons who continued the tradition up until the end of the century.

If that's not enough, John's brothers, Sameal and Solomon also entered the family business. They were in partnership, in fact, from 1833 in Strasburg, Virginia. The factory they founded ran until 1908.

Pottery of the Midwest

No single style and no single type of clay can describe the pottery that potters of the Midwest region turned out in the 19th century. From Ohio into Indiana, it's an eclectic mix of wares.

Among the most abundant of items included a washbowl and jug, glazed a buff color inside. On the one handle of the jug a stamp indicates "Zoar". On the other handle is the date of 1840. The piece was made by a religious group called the Society of Separatists or Zoarites.

This group was really just one of many religious sects which formed communal settlements during this time. (A group similar to this formed in Oneida, NY, from which we still have Oneida silverware.)

Originally, this group came from Württemberg. They prospered from 1819 to nearly 1898 in an Ohio town called Zoar in Tuscarawas County. Pottery is not the only craft these people practiced, either. The commune had weavers and carpenters, as well as its own print shop and bindery, and a blacksmith shop.

Eventually pottery came into it own in the budding country. But due to the very practical nature of the young nation, the residents didn't feel the "need" nor could they afford some of the more elaborate or decorative items that the English and continental Europeans seems to demand.

The result was a fairly slow growing, rather utilitarian look in pieces. In many cases that also meant that many of the items looked, well, rather mundane -- with the exception of the colorful nature of the Pennsylvania Dutch.

Want to discover more about this marvelous hobby of antiques? Another popular object of antique collectors everywhere is furniture. And that just happens to be our next stop along this amazing antique journey!

PART 3: STALKING THE GREAT MAHOGANY (AND OAK AND WALNUT, TOO)

If you think pursuing pottery is confusing, wait until you get started on your Great Furniture Hunt. Welcome to the world of Queen Anne, William and Mary and Tudor.

You'll also learn about the differences between oak, mahogany, and walnut -- and the difference between American walnut and English walnut.

Oh, I know it makes your head spin right now, but for the veteran antique hunter, it's a dream come true. Very soon, you'll understand what makes it so attractive to collector.

CHAPTER 7- ENGLISH FURNITURE - WELCOME TO THE MAZE!

It's the birthplace of some of our earliest leaders. It's what colored our nature in those vital colonial years -- England. The earliest settlers came from England, so it's no surprise that English furniture plays such a remarkably important role for so many antique collectors to this day.

While American furniture has a rich history all on it's own, we're delving into English first, because for the longest time -- some 300 years ago-- American-made furniture was just a duplication of what was being made in England. There's just one catch, though. The duplication happened some 50 years after that fact. But I'm getting ahead of myself. Let's take a closer look at this maze of styles.

Lost in the woods . . . of English furniture

Where do you even begin in trying to pin down the many incredible facets of English furniture? For many collectors, the simplest wa is to classify it by the type of wood from which it's made.

No, it's not a foolproof method,. There is indeed overlap among the four distinct groups. But it is probably one of the easiest ways to learn about English furniture. And from there, we can talk about the different styles.

If you choose to collect it, of course, you'll soon immerse yourself not only in the varieties of woods from which they're made, but also the different periods as well as the makers of these fine pieces.

Oak: A hard look at a hard wood

Not only is oak very hard and resists decay and woodworm, it's traditionally English in nature. It was the sole source of furniture in England until approximately 1630. Other types of woods have been added throughout the years and, as you're about to see, still used today for the creation of fine furniture.

During the height of its popularity, the homes of those who could afford such furniture were large. In fact, the main room, referred to as "the hall,' was more often than not enormous.

In response, the furniture of the era was also big. If you think you're going to find small pieces of 16th Century English furniture, you're bound to be disappointed. And, if on the off chance that you do find a small piece or two, be prepared to spend quite a bit of money if you want to add it to your collection.

You'll also discover that oak furniture of this time period was also made in continental Europe and resembles the English style as well.

Walnut

Attractive, light brown with beautiful dark patterns, walnut came into its own in the late 17th century. While much of it was homegrown in England, a surprisingly large amount was also imported from other countries -- especially France.

Many furniture makers enjoyed working with the French variety of walnut wood. They claim that it possessed more attractive markings.

You'll find some solid pieces of walnut furniture, but for the most part, it's used as a thin veneer, glued down to the main piece of furniture. This practice enabled the furniture craftsmen to be discriminatory. In this manner they were able to use only the best marked pieces of wood and to also arrange them in patterns that were most pleasing to the eye.

The most familiar of these is called "quartering". No doubt you've seen it but didn't realize what it was called. In this practice, four successively cut rectangular pieces are arranged in such a fashion that their markings correspond evenly. Just as popular as these was a pattern labeled as "oysters", These are circular pieces cut across a branch.

The great walnut tree shortage of 1709

Who cares? I can hear you ask now. You are probably only really concerned if you plan on collecting English furniture. But, read on even if you're not collecting English furniture, because this is a grand example of how historical events may well affect your patterns of collecting -- even some 300 years after the fact. Who knew?

The harsh winter of 1709 destroyed a large number of walnut trees, not only in England but across the entire European continent. In its place, the craftsmen substituted American walnut, which is very similar -- but not exact. In some instances the two species are barely distinguishable.

On the other hand, some pieces of American walnut have fewer natural markings. This oftentimes causes even collectors with the most discriminating eyes to confuse it with mahogany when that wood was first being introduced in the decade from 1730 to 1740.

The rise of mahogany

With the rise of mahogany around approximately 1730, walnut quickly fell into disfavor. But its fall from grace, as it were, had more to do with the introduction of central heating perhaps than the advantages of mahogany, per se.

Interested? Here's another instance where history meets antiquing head on. For example, at one time, Queen Anne walnut furniture enjoyed immense popularity. When central heat was introduced into the more exclusive homes, though, people noticed that the walnut veneer of the furniture fell off, precisely due, they finally figured, to the heat. Veneered furniture became disliked practically overnight.

Mahogany needs no introduction. We're all familiar with the reddish brown wood. It's as popular today in furniture making as it was when it was first introduced in 1730.

Usually the wood was imported from any number of countries especially from Honduras, the Bahamas, San Domingo and Cuba.

The key here is that these geographical locations often produced woods that weren't technically mahogany, even though they were near the color of the wood. The term eventually took on the broader meaning to describe any wood of that reddish- brown color.

Mahogany possesses many advantages, not the least of which is its strength. It's also resistant to warping and splitting. And much to the surprise -- and indeed the pleasure -- of many craftsmen, mahogany can be found in large enough pieces that a large table top could be fashioned out of it without the need for joining smaller pieces together. Believe it or not, this one-piece table top had never been possible before.

Satinwood's 30-year history

1780-1810. If you discover a piece of antique English furniture made of Satinwood these are the years it was most likely created. Native to both the East and West Indies, Satinwood is distinguished by a warm yellow color and a close grain that polishes to a high shine. For the most part it was used as a veneer, but it had to be handled gently otherwise it would split.

Around 1800, it was introduced in solid form as a material for the manufacturing of chairs as well as the legs of veneered tables. The cost of this particular wood, however, meant that only the wealthiest of families could afford it.

There were two popular ways to decorate this wood. The first was to have it inlaid with other light-colored woods. The second -- and usually the most widely used -- was to paint designs on it with oil-based paint. The designs were normally small bouquets of flowers as well as garlands of trailing leaves.

In addition to these four major varieties of woods used you can distinguish English furniture by the different styles used throughout the ages.

Tudor: 1558-1603 Elizabeth I to James I

Oak. Of course the furniture of this period was built of oak. The style is called Tudor because that was the name of the reigning royal family during this time period.

The construction, you'll discover, was anything but elaborate. The mortice and tenon joint were snugly held with a dowel or a wooden peg. The most noticeable features of the Tudor style are the exaggerated bulbous turned legs on tables and bedstead posts as well as on the supports of the front of cupboards.

Jacobean: 1603-1647 James I to Cromwell

It was during this time period that walnut was introduced to the world through craftsmen. It's hard to say how much walnut furniture was actually produced at the time, but it may very well be much more than we realize. Unfortunately, woodworm may have destroyed much of it.

Additionally, Jacobean pieces seldom include the bulbous support unlike the pieces created during the preceding Tudor time period.

Cromwellian: 1649-1660 Oliver and Richard Cromwell

Getting a feeling for furniture styles here? They are remarkably aligned with the leadership of the country. And so it is with this third category we're reviewing: Cromwellian.

During this period the principal woods used were oak and walnut. The most distinguishing characteristic of the Cromwellian period is the turned ornament.

Fronts of chests were decorated with turned columns. Usually, the columns were cut into two halves lengthwise, then inlaid with simple patterns in materials such as bone, mother of pearl, or ivory.

On chairs and legs of tables, the turning was often in a series of knobs, which eventually became known as "bobbin-turning." Additionally, during this period, it was not unusual to find the seats of some chairs to be made of leather with large brass-headed nails.

Carolean 1660-1689 Charles II to the Flight of James II

Historically, the pendulum often swings. And sometimes it sweeps with a wider arc than others. This period marks a very wide sweeping change from the era before it.

The era of the Cromwells was also characterized by the rise of Puritans. And that, as you can well imagine, was marked by a design that was austere, simple and well, yes, plain and functional.

Enter Charles II. No sooner does he appears on the historical English scene, does that pendulum begin to move faster than you can say "Goodbye, Mayflower!" The entire tone of the country -- at least in the way of furniture -- appeared to change overnight. "Austere" as a concept was swept out the door. Luxury and extravagance were invited in.

Walnut, for one thing, overtook the furniture industry. Oh, you could still find some oak furniture being made, but not as much as before.

Meet the new "standard" decorations

Veneers, marquetry, and lacquers (not to be confused with the delightfully intoxicating liquors) were now for the most part standard decorations. Another characteristic of this age is the silver embossing on furniture. Nothing austere about any of this!

The tall-backed chair, while used in an earlier era, was re-introduced and new life was breathed into it. As you might guess, it was offered in a more elaborate fashion. In fact, it eventually became the typical feature of the Carolean period. Both the back and front rails of the chair were carved quite elaborately. The most popular design being used? A pair of cherub angels holding a crown. Both the seat and the back were caned.

William and Mary: 1689-1702

Ah! Now we're talking complications for the antique collector. And once again, it's wrapped up in these vignettes of history. If you're beginning to notice that being an antique collector also means being familiar with at least some portion of history. . .BINGO! You're absolutely right.

And here's the problem you'll run smack dab into when you decide to collect English furniture from this time period.

King William III was also the Prince of Orange. He became King by marrying Queen Mary, daughter of James II, the former king of England. (Keep this in mind because it's important.) William was born and raised in Holland.

When "Bill" came over from Holland, a large number of Dutch workers followed him. It's not unusual that he -- and his queen by the way -- were fonder of Dutch furniture than the traditional English furniture.

So it may also come as no surprise that during this time period, 1689 to approximately 1702, it may be difficult to tell the English-crafted items from the Dutch.

A few more complications thrown in

But if you think that's the only complication this era brings, you're mistaken. If that weren't enough, it's also difficult to tell the pieces manufactured during the William and Mary period from those of the following era -- Queen Anne style (1702-1744).

Pieces with elaborate decorations are usually considered to have been made prior to the year 1700. Many of the cabinets and chests of the era possessed a simple, plain, turned ball-shaped foot as well as turned legs.

Additionally, cross-connecting pieces, which brought the legs of chairs and tables together called stretchers, were -- for a lack of a better term, a "wavy" shape. They usually also possessed a pointed turned finial or knob at the location where the pieces physically crossed each other and chairs.

Queen Anne: 1702-1714

Hear the phrase "Queen Anne" and think walnut. Well, if you don't now, you certainly will as you become more familiar with this furniture style. And here's another piece of knowledge you'll learn quickly enough: some of the best surviving pieces date from the Queen Anne period. Now that's a fact that you can easily take to the bank (if you were so inclined!)

You'll seldom see marquetry used in furniture of this era, even though lacquer remained quite popular. The most important introduction that most antique collectors agree on was the introduction of the cabriole leg. Very often it was carved with a shell or the fat curved knee.

In other interior décor trends of this time, mirrors were gaining in popularity, even as they shrunk in size. Another standard feature of the Queen Anne era was upholstery along with both silk and needlepoint.

Early Georgian: 1714-1730 or 1740

Ah! Another era that's easy to mistake for Queen Anne. This period, marked a rise in gilding, which was used with enthusiasm for the frames of mirrors as well as on tables and chairs.

In addition, the Kent or Palladian style was fashionable. Named after William Kent, a prominent architect of the time, this trend revealed itself very often in the broken pediment as a feature of marble table tops.

Mid-Georgian Chippendale 1730 or 1740 to 1770

Okay ladies, listen up. This is the Chippendale era in furniture, not the modern Chippendale male dancers. Keep those motel keys in your purses, please!

Now things are getting a bit confusing. For starters, you'll discover that this era is marked by the use of three completely different types of woods. For a very brief time red walnut -- from across the Atlantic in Virginia -- was used primarily in the crafting of furniture. That was replaced by French walnut. And then, before 1770, mahogany was introduced.

Initially, mahogany simply replaced walnut as the wood of choice. All the same styles of furniture were still being churned out by the master craftsmen. But, of course, nothing could ever be just that simple, now could it?

Craftsmen soon came to love how easy it was to work with mahogany, and they found themselves using it more often.

The hodge-podge of Chippendale

Grouped under this broad umbrella term "Chippendale", an inquisitive collector of antiques finds almost a hodge-podge of various designs.

Again the answer to why this came to be can easily be found by rooting through a little history. If you do dig a little deeper, you discover a cabinet-maker by the name of Thomas Chippendale. Not only did this man collect the different styles of this era, he adapted and documented them as well. The resulting project produced a book entitled, The Director, which was published in 1754.

That's why just about every piece of furniture made from 1750 to 1780 is known as a "Chippendale." And that's why, now well on your way to being a savvy, knowledgeable antiques collector, you won't be in the least surprised to find a wide variety of furniture styles grouped under this embracing category.

Need to break all of this down just a little more?

When you hear the term French Chippendale, think curves and cabriole legs with a toe curling outward. Gothic Chippendale most notably reveals a lancet-shaped, pointed top on furniture or even on the doors for bookcases. In addition, the form of piercing for the back of many chairs and the fretting on chairs is indicative of this period.

Chinese Chippendale is probably the easiest to recognize. Yes, it's covered with all things Chinese. Think pagodas, Chinese figures, birds, and the whole Chinese motif many of us love so well. Usually on the furniture, the Chinese symbols are limited to just one per piece. But for the frames of mirrors, the craftsmen usually included all of the various symbols.

Later Georgian 1770-1810 Adam, Hepplewhite and Sheraton

The forty years from 1770 to 1810 saw several styles come and go. When a collector refers to Adam in this period, he's speaking about the Adam brothers, Robert and James. Architects by profession, they took delight in designing in general -- even furniture.

As a testament to their passion, they not only designed their homes (you and I might refer to them as mansions), but the interior design of the mansions as well. They also went one step further by creating the concepts of the furniture they wanted to see occupy that space.

You may be relieved to know that as talented as they were, they drew the line at actually crafting the furniture themselves. But they did assign this task to one of the most respected craftsmen of their time. You guessed it again -- Thomas Chippendale. Who else?

The next style is the Hepplewhite. A cabinet maker, George Hepplewhite, from which we get the name of this style, created pieces of furniture that were rather simple in nature as well as small physically compared to what came before.

One of the most well-known of his pieces is a chair with a back that is heart-shaped or shield-shaped. On some pieces the shield also has a pierced and carved Prince of Wales feather.

The final style of the Later Georgian period is that of Sheraton, named after Thomas Sheraton. Sheraton introduced furniture containing a more slender line than had been created before. He also re-introduced the use of inlay. It's this inlay, in fact, that he's most noted for.

This feature very often consisted of cross banding and stringing. In addition, Sheraton added an oval shell made of satinwood to his pieces. The shell, surprisingly was scorched. In this way, it looked as if it were shaded.

By the 1800s Sheraton replaced the famous square legs with turned ones with reeding.

Regency: 1800-1820

Again, if you collect furniture from this period, you'll notice that it's a combination of three styles. The first is the Greek and Roman style. And there's no mistaking why it's labeled this. The furniture is adorned with figures of mythological gods and goddesses. In addition, when you see a piece from this time period, look down at the legs. More often than not you'll see a lion's paw.

An extremely interesting theme in this period is the lyre. And this shows up, of all places, in end tables. The tables themselves are shaped liked lyres.

The second theme in the Regency era is the Egyptian one. It makes use of sphinxes as well as the classic Egyptian head for the tops of columns. Ah, but the creativity doesn't stop with the top of the column. The theme continues to the bottom of the column. Look down and the chances are great that you'll find an Egyptian foot at the bottom of that column.

This style also uses one more symbol of ancient Egypt, that of the crocodile.

And finally, you'll find a Chinese flavor to some of the furniture in this period. Unmistakably Chinese, in fact. The Regency saw the use of all types of Chinese patterns, shapes and colors. The most vivid example of Chinese influence can be seen in the pavilion at Brighton.

The era of many woods

Along with these various styles, you'll also discover that woods of unusual types were used in addition to the standard mahogany. Inlay consisted mostly of brass and mounts utilized gilt bronze.

The Chinese style also saw physically smaller chairs being crafted. But that is far from the sole distinguishing feature of this style. In the early Regency period, the chairs had legs that curved in such a way that they appeared to be sabers. And indeed, that's the name the legs were given. Later in the period the legs were turned.

William IV Early Victorian 1820-1840

It's easy to confuse the furniture made in this time period with that of the Regency, even for the veteran antique collectors.

The problem revolves around the simple fact that many of the designs are similar. Of course, if you take a little closer look, you'll notice that during this period, the furniture is heavier. Not only that, but the chairs and tables of this era as well as other pieces are actually coarser looking and appear to be nothing if not "clumsy" looking.

Another telltale difference is in the leg style. Gone are the sabre legs of the Regency period. Most of the furniture produced in this time period has turned supports and very often they're tapered and carved turned supports

We've just examined English-craft antique furniture from several different angles. Now it's time to confuse and confound you just a bit more with the addition of the styles of the European continent. Hold on! You're in for a wonderfully exciting ride!

CHAPTER 8- CONTINENTAL EUROPEAN FURNITURE - A MYRIAD OF STYLES

As you might suspect, the most well-known pieces of continental European furniture can be found among the French craftsmen. But depending on the period pieces you're examining, you may be surprised that distinguishing a French design from an Italian design is more difficult than you thought.

French furniture: Never came cheap

French furniture. To some -- antique collectors and laymen alike -- it represents the height of the antique avocation. The cream of the crop if you will.

In many ways, that is a very accurate description. Even when brand new, it proved to be an expensive purchase. Don't expect to find many rock bottom prices here.

Yet, for all of the expense and the distinction with which we take notice of it now, who knew that even this classic at one time suffered from an identity crisis?

In this case, I'm talking 16th and 17th Century pieces. Oh don't worry about separating it from the English styles, you'll have no trouble there. Your problem may develop when you try to tell it apart from the rest of the furniture on the European continent at that time

Let me warn you though, that even when set side-by-side, English and French pieces are remarkably similar. The main difference between the two? The English items are made from oak. The French pieces, in contrast, are made with walnut wood native to France.

If that doesn't confuse you, the fact that French pieces look like the rest of the continent might. But, then again there is good reason for this. Paris during this time period was a magnet for foreign craftsman, each bringing the style of his native homeland to the city.

Yes, it technically was made in France, making it a French piece, but it was created by a craftsman who may have called

Italy or Germany his home. And he was undoubtedly making furniture that reflects that fact.

By the end of the 17th Century, however, a singular French style emerged. And it was created by Andre Charles Boulle. It's no surprise then that it's known as Boulle work, or in some circles you'll see it referred to Buhl work. He perfected a marquetry which used both tortoise shell and brass. This device was found on furniture veneered with ebony.

Louis XV

Perhaps the most extravagant of all designs, Rococo, was a style that quickly spread throughout all of Europe. Literally meaning decorated with shells and scrollwork, this particular style is also known for its curves as well as what can only be called an "unbalanced" look.

Your first impression of Louis XV furniture may be that it's nothing if it's not "showy." Indeed, in our 21st Century world, it really does stand out as that. But when you view it in the venue from which it was created, it really does look quite "at home."

French furniture during the 18th Century included a particular taste for small tables and cabinets as well as chests of drawers most commonly called commodes. (Yep! You read that correctly!)

In addition, this period also favored large writing tables characterized by leather-covered tops. These tables are also notable for having a row of drawers beneath the table top and legs that were actually quite long.

Another popular piece at this time was an upright cabinet possessing a drop down front. When the front was raised it appeared to be a cabinet, but when you dropped the front, it created a nice spacious writing area.

For any type of decoration in the Louis XV era think veneer, but not just any veneer. Think veneer plus marquetry and parquetry set off with ormolu mountings. Ormolu, an alloy of copper, tin and zinc, created a gold look that was used for many decorative purposes.

Louis XVI

This furniture is so called because its popularity can be gauged roughly the French monarch's reign from 1774-1793. Straight lines are now the trend. Gone are the curves of the Rococo period. Tables and cabinets now have square, not rounded corners. Their legs were square or rounded -- anything but the cabriole style of old.

Veneer and ormolu mounting, though, still remained popular. Many pieces during this time were also decorated with Sevres porcelain. In many instances, in fact, the porcelain itself was painted in the distinctive blue and white to resemble Wedgewood ware.

Empire

With the excesses of the French Revolution dying away, the 18th Century ushered in a style of austerity in French furniture (relatively speaking, of course!). Plain mahogany furniture became fashionable. Its color was darker and carried more grain than that of the same wood used in England.

Inlay, when it did exist, consisted of brass with restrained ormolu mounts.

Beware the "genuine reproductions"

Yes, the "Genuine Reproduction" is greatly evident when you deal in French furniture. Since French antique furniture is expensive -- and was expensive even before it became an antique -- and the demand has remained high, the reproduction market in this area is very healthy. Don't let it fool you!

One custom that you may already be familiar with is that of stamping French-made articles with the craftsman's name. Don't assume that just because you've found a stamp, that it automatically makes it authentic. When the reproductions were being made, the creators duplicated even the smallest of details, including the stamp!

German Furniture

If it looks like Queen Anne, but with a little more added extravagance. It's probably a piece of furniture crafted in Germany.

While an English chest may possess a gently shaped front with straight sides, a similar German piece may have a deeply curved front with curved sides instead.

Holland

Here's another case where "mistaken identity" may prevail if you're not careful. Dutch and English furniture have always appeared similar. You'll also find the same holds true for Dutch and Flemish oak pieces.

If you recall, we briefly mentioned the influx of Dutch craftsmen into England during the eras of both William & Mary and Queen Anne. So, this should really come as no surprise.

You can distinguish some of the Dutch-made pieces from the English because the Dutch are "over-shaped" and contains more decorations than the English-made versions.

As you delve deeper into the hobby, you may discover Dutch-made chairs that look as if they were made by Englishman Robert Adam. They have carved ornaments of leaves and ribbons created from mahogany.

And you may find Dutch manufactured cupboards created from walnut and ebony just about anywhere. These cupboards, with two large doors, were made specifically for overseas travel. So there's no telling where they may show up.

During the later part of the 18th Century, Dutch cabinetmakers created furniture featuring oak veneered along with satinwood. These pieces, additionally, were inset with shaped panels of lacquer.

You can also find tables, cabinets and full-front secretaries in this style. Some of the walnut and mahogany furniture from this country has been inlaid with marquetry of flowers and birds. Bookcases and sloping front bureaus have also been described this way.

But many times, decorative items were added after the original creation of the object, during an era when "plain" furniture was not particularly fashionable.

Italy

There is no single national Italian design. You'll discover every district had its own unique style. And you'll also discover Italian craftsmen shared many of the same techniques as their continental brethren.

Scandinavia

Now, there's a complication for you as an antique hunter. It was not uncommon for English furniture to be imported into Scandinavia in the 18th Century.

For authentic Scandinavian furniture look to the name of George Haupt. Trained in both London and Paris, Haupt worked in Stockholm, specializing in the style of Louis XVI. Discover an authentic piece by Haupt and you've pulled off an antique coup. His work is rare -- and it goes without saying, it's valuable.

Congratulations! You've covered both English and continental European furniture like a professional. Are you ready to learn your way around a roomful of American-made furniture? Don't worry. It gets easier as we go along!

CHAPTER 9- FOLLOWING THE TRAIL OF AMERICAN FURNITURE

I can see it in your eyes. You're thinking about pulling off the ultimate antique furniture coup. Now don't kill the messenger, but let me just save you some, time, money and effort. If the antique furniture you're hunting was made in America, don't bother to take a trip abroad hoping to find some long hidden treasure. Chances are slim to none that you'll find anything.

And yes, I can state this with relative confidence. Very little -- if any -- antique American furniture is actually discovered outside of this country. You can't even find examples of them on display at museums anywhere in Europe.

That is not to say the occasional piece doesn't come along. But more often than not, it's snatched up by a quick, responsive and moneyed collector. These occasional pieces have been brought back -- usually to England -- by early American settlers who decided that the colonial living was not their cup of tea.

When these rare pieces are put up for auction, they usually sell for exorbitant prices compared to similar pieces made in

England around the same time. But there are good reasons for this.

The first of these is that antique American furniture is rarer than English antique furniture. That makes sense. There were far fewer colonists living across the ocean than English living in England.

Not only that, but what American furniture that does exist is already either in the hands of collectors or well-guarded by American museums.

And as we learned earlier, the demand is present for such pieces. You'll find plenty of collectors willing to fight over these few pieces. That always drives the price up.

So what am I looking for?

Presumably, you're looking in the United States for this furniture. If it's 17th Century furniture you're searching for, then it will look remarkably like English furniture crafted 50 years earlier. Honestly. It will.

This simple time lag, by the way, continues throughout the majority of the 18th Century as well. By 1800 though, the gap begins to close. Conditions were improving in the New Country. And shipping capabilities between the two countries were increasing.

By 1800, in fact, a visitor to the United States could see little difference between the décor of a fashionable New York City mansion and that of one in London.

Of course, you expect nothing less. The vast majority of the settlers of the New World were from England. It's only natural they would copy the fashionable furniture of that country.

The "localization" of American furniture

But American furniture makers added yet another twist. And this was the ability to "localize" pieces. Take the Jacobean cane-backed chair. It was reproduced in all parts of the colonies. It was extremely popular -- but not identical. And the differences depended on the geographic locations of origin.

The traditional chairs possessed a back filled with a panel of caning. In certain locations of America though, craftsmen gave the chair a series of shaped uprights. And before you know it, you witnessed the birth of the "banister-back" chair.

Similarly, with the introduction of mahogany, craftsmen in Newport, Rhode Island created straight-front kneehole desks and chests that had a "block front." This is a kind of break-front of a serpentine shape. One or more of the flat blocks are carved with a sunray or shell.

Variations of this particular chair did, indeed, become popular in the area, but never really caught on in other areas.

Every district had its own personality when it came to furniture. But perhaps the most famous of these was the city of Philadelphia, the City of Brotherly Love. Chests, tables and chairs are of definite mid-18th Century design. But when you examine the carving and fretwork, you realize none of the construction came from London.

By the first half of the 19th Century, Americanized Sheraton furniture gained favor. Especially loved was the work of Duncan Phyfe. A native of Scotland, Phyfe is undoubtedly the most well-known and best-loved of all American cabinet makers.

He created items that were in the style of late-Sheraton as well as another style called Directoire.

Some antique collectors, due to the overlap of various styles in this era, have lumped these two styles with several other designs. These are referred to as Early Empire.

Don't overlook country charm

Bustling cities like Boston or Philadelphia weren't the only areas producing furniture. Rural areas, too, were home to some fine craftsmanship. Again, it's no surprise these pieces imitated those from Europe, and not just England.

By the 19th Century, it was not uncommon to find immigrants from countries other than England in the newly established United States. Of these, the most distinctive group was the German settler. Living mostly in eastern Pennsylvania, these people quickly became known as the Pennsylvania Germans or more popularly called today, Pennsylvania Dutch. They decorated their homes with items of almost exclusively light-colored fruit woods.

Into the woods

It's not just the design of the American pieces that makes it different from its English counterparts, but the wood from which it's made. Many of the American pieces are made of woods indigenous to their localized area. Apple and cherry are seen frequently, as is walnut. It's not unusual to find a great example of American-made Chippendale. But instead of it being crafted out of mahogany, as it would be in England, you may find it's made of walnut or even cherry.

What's in a name?

Here is another difference from English-made and American-crafted pieces: the names. Indeed, as the American culture evolved, so did the language used to describe furniture.

In England what was referred to as a dressing table was more commonly called a lowboy on the other side of the Atlantic.

And it's fairly descriptive. It is, indeed, a low table with drawers.

A highboy, is merely a lowboy with what the English would call a chest of drawers sitting on top of it.

Now, here is where it can get confusing, especially if you're new to the Great Antique Hunt. An English-labeled chest of drawers alone became a bureau in America. But the English did have a piece called a bureau. But it wasn't that. In America, an English-labeled bureau was widely known as a slant-front desk.

The new country also had a piece of furniture called the secretary. Go over to England and look for a bureau-bookcase. And you've discovered it. It's a sloping front writing desk with a bookcase on top.

Continuing along this line...

Let's talk about another piece of furniture that gained popular during the late 19th century and turned into a "generic" term of sorts in some parts of the country by the early 20th century. That's the davenport. Think you know what it means?

Then you may be surprised to learn that this simple word actually applies to two different pieces of furniture -- developed a century and an ocean apart from the other. Yes, it is an interesting story.

Let's start with the American definition of davenport. Originally, it denoted a sofa that was rather square looking with a high back and arms. The style, resembling a box in many ways, developed around the turn of the century. It's named for the A.H. Davenport Co. of Boston.

Soon the term came to be used with any sofa or couch, especially in upstate New York and the Midwest. In fact, the term was so popular, that when sofa-beds were first introduced, they were dubbed "davenport beds."

But that's far from the end of the story. The Kroehler Company of Naperville, IL became the first furniture company to actually patent a sofa containing a hidden mattress and springs in 1909. This type of sofa was so popular, in fact, that the word davenport came to mean any foldout bed.

Introducing the British davenport!

And now let's take a quick trip across the Atlantic to see what the British called a davenport. I'll give you a hint: it wasn't a sofa! In fact, their davenport was a small desk, one with a slanted or pull-out top. It also contained a row of drawers down one, if not both sides.

Originally, the term was used to describe a simple chest of drawers with a swivel top. But as the piece of furniture evolved, it was made with hidden compartments and various cubbyholes of sorts.

This davenport originates from the 1790s. Developed by a furniture firm called Gillow's based in Lancaster, England, the name itself comes from the name of the company's client, believe it or not, a "Captain Davenport." If Captain Davenport wanted this unique piece of furniture for a specific reason, it's lost in history.

But that doesn't stop antique collectors from thinking that it might have been quite convenient to take with him on various military campaigns or onboard ships. Eventually, this uniquely commissioned item because a standard piece of English 19th century furniture.

We've just got a quick glance at the varieties of antique furniture. There's a wide assortment for your collection, if you are so inclined and have the money to invest. Our next section deals with glassware. This area, just like the other two, can be confusing in attempting to distinguish different eras, the origins of countries and the original creators of the pieces. But this is also where a little knowledge goes a long way.

PART 4: GRABBING GLASSWARE

We've covered pottery and furniture. Now it's time we scrutinize the origins of antique glass. As you well may imagine, it's not an easy hunt. Your quest for glassware may have you more puzzled than satisfied.

But there's one thing I know for sure - in the process of identifying and classifying glass, you'll experience the journey of a lifetime.

Once again, we break the trip into three separate stops: English, continental Europe and American. Come on and enjoy the ride!

Chapter 10- I'll Drink to That! With the Fine Glassware of Europe

Venice. The epitome of glassmaking. Venice. The home of hundreds of years of glassmaking knowledge and expertise. Venice. Innovator and leader and bastion of everything dealing with glass.

Okay, so perhaps with the last sentence we're getting a little carried away. But I'm betting there are some antique hunters, collectors and lovers of find glass who would probably agree with me even on that last sentence.

The point of the paragraph is to illustrate that the history of Venice in crafting this material includes an unbroken timeline that harkens back to at least several hundred years.

Consider this: the master craftsmen of Venice recreated a technique called latticino. An ability lost since the time of the ancient Egyptians and Romans, it was the method of embedding threads of white or colored glass into clear glass.

The creation of the clear glass itself, called cristallo, was a triumph of the Venice glassmaking community.

Glass created with lacelike patterns displayed a skill of remarkably precise mathematical knowledge. But that's not the only method the Venetian glassmakers used to decorate their products.

Enamels were painted on the glass -- much like the painting of Chinaware -- and then fired. Certain pieces displayed gilding and still others were engraved.

Very often the white glassware used as decoration in the latticino pieces was used independently as well. When used alone, they bore an uncanny resemblance to porcelain.

Soon, though, the Venetian glass trade declined. Other countries were beginning to learn to create their own high-quality products. Venice-originated creations may have slowed, but it never stopped.

During the greater part of the 16th and 17th centuries, Venice craftsmen discovered more ways to keep working. They became the finest creators of mirror glass. They really were years ahead of their time.

As partial proof of this, you'll no doubt notice if you study antique glass for very long, that early Venetian styles makes a resurgence in the Victorian age. Truly, that's a testimonial to their classic beauty.

But the classic "timelessness" of these pieces poses a problem for the antique collector. Exactly. Our job is to take these pieces out of that realm of "timelessness" and label it with a date of creation. The resurgence makes the collector's job that much more difficult.

The Dutch: Diamond engraving

Oh, sure, said the Dutch confidently. Anyone can imitate Venetian glass making. But can they do this?

And with that question, they decorated the glass in the way that . . . well . . . only the Dutch (or so they thought!) could. During the 18th and 19th centuries, they -- like the Germans -

- decorated a large portion of their production by cutting it on the wheel.

Their specialty, though, entailed engraving with a diamond. So finely executed were the pieces, that many times, the engraving went unnoticed until light gently fell across the pieces of glass.

You can find engraved pieces as early as 1600 from the Ruksmusem in Amsterdam, but similar work shows up later in the that century as well as the 18th century. Of those who practiced this fine art, two of the most prolific craftsmen were Frans Greenwood and David Wolff.

By now, it shouldn't surprise you to discover that much of their work is neither signed nor dated. (Don't give up on your quest to find signed and dated work by these gentlemen. Some really do exist!)

Since many others in Holland were performing similar work, sorting all of this out gets just a bit tricky at times.

As you progress in your pursuit of antiques, you may encounter the name of Zuener. Working at the end of the 18th century, he actually painted on glass -- and with a unique style. Not only did he use gold and silver leaf lace on the back of the glass, but he then scratched through this and filled it in with black paint. The skies in his outdoor scenes were painted naturally. The effect is nothing if not stunning.

France

Prior to the end of the 18th century, French glassware plays no real role in adding to either the quality or standards of the art. Up until this time, the French glass makers concentrated on making stained glass for churches.

French glass ware didn't develop its own "personality" until the end of the 18th century. Factories then operated with the mission "to make products in the manner and quality of England."

One of the first factories to appear, was located at Luneville, in 1765. Two years later, in 1767, another establishment opened by the Cristallerie de St. Louis in Lorraine.

These factories developed a singular style of encasing white ceramic medallions in clear crystal. This gave the objects a beautiful silver appearance. Among the pieces created in this fashion are paperweights and goblets.

Another variation on this theme was the creation of clear-glass paperweights decorated within colored canes of the same material. Not only was this style of paperweight made in the two factories already mentioned, but also in a third in Clichy.

As an antique collector, you may run into them. You'll recognize them by their markings. Dated mostly from 1845 to 1849, each of these carries an initial indicating the factor of origin. "B" indicates it was made at Baccarat. If the piece is marked with a "C", it was created at Clichy and "SL" stands for St. Louis.

The dates on the paperweights -- and yes, really there are dates on them -- are never placed in the center of the object. In fact, many times, they're a hunt in and of themselves.

As with any other potentially valuable collectible, it should come as no surprise that these items have been forged throughout the years. But you won't fall prey to these fakes if you keep in mind that the fake pieces are not as clear as the real deal!

Now that you have had a quick tour of some European glassware (yes, we could write a book -- several books -- on this topic), lets skip over to England, where those craftsmen were also busy producing quality pieces.

CHAPTER 11- CLEARLY A RICH HISTORY - GLASSMAKERS OF ENGLAND

Are you thinking of buying that piece of glassware? Why, yes, it certainly is beautiful. But don't you think it's a bit expensive? Can you tell me what that piece of glass is? Its original function? Its origin? No?

If you're buying that particular glass purely because it appeals to your senses, and you don't mind the seemingly hefty price tag, go ahead. But, if you're purchasing it as an antique investment, I'd think again.

That's not to say that it wouldn't be a good investment. All I'm saying right now is that you don't have enough information about it to really know how it will work out as an investment.

Just like furniture and pottery, or any other antique, you're always a smarter collector and a shrewder bargainer if you know the history of the object you intend to purchase.

Glass: Clearly a rich history

Glassmaking, of course, is an ancient art. The most ancient of these pieces are already carefully locked away in museums for the public to view. It's still vital, though, to at least have a passing familiarity with glassware's illustrious ancient past.

The residents of the Roman Empire actually conquered and perfected the fine art of glassmaking. Perhaps nothing better represents these skills than the Tear Bottle. This is a small bottle, which due to its being buried for so very long, has an iridescent luster to it.

Of course, you won't find any examples of these Roman treasures at your local antique store. To find an engaging item like this, you would need to visit a museum.

When the Roman Empire fell, the art of glassmaking fell with it. It was harder -- but not impossible -- to find beautiful, high-quality glass after that.

You just had to look to the Near East, in order to discover glass. Persia as well as several other countries were making glass, especially between the seventh and eleventh centuries.

In the years to follow, Syria produced amazing glass pieces, including mosque lamps and vases. At the same time, low bowls and cups began to be seen. Made from green and brown-colored glass, these bottles differed from the ones the Romans had made. The ancient Romans had included what's called a foot on every vessel, which was artfully joined to the jar itself. This foot is not found on ancient English vessels, however.

Now on to the English

Good quality glass was produced in Roman-occupied England. Once the occupiers pulled up stakes, so to speak, and left, very few quality glassmakers were left in that country.

Of course, as the years evolved so did the quality of the glass. Glassmakers honed their craft and two cities actually became known for its fine quality in this area: Surrey and Sussex.

Otherwise, the glassware made during this period was for purely utilitarian purposes. Of course, several cities specialized strictly in making stained glass for churches.

During much of the 16th century, England depended on glass imported from Venice, Italy. Other needs were amply supplied by Italian workers living in London. Many of these immigrants did not make England their permanent home, however.

Queen Elizabeth I And Verzelini

In 1575, the playing field changed. Queen Elizabeth I granted Jacopo Verzelini what was known as a "privilege." During the 21 years of this grant, Verzelini would make Venice-style glass in London as well as teach the art to Englishman.

Simultaneously, the importation of glass from Venice was prohibited -- at least by formal law. Whether some still came through is a matter of speculation to many antique collectors.

For 70 years after that first grant, a series of individuals held similar government-issued monopolies for glassmaking. It was also during this period that wood was replacing coal as burning material for heating furnaces.

Much of the English-produced glass created during this time period is of such high quality that it's difficult to tell it apart from the Italian-made pieces.

There is one exception to this blanket statement. English-produced wine bottles from the 17th century on. The particular pieces, included a circular glass seal on the shoulder of the bottle. This seal showed the name of the owner and the date. Many of these have, indeed, survived throughout the years.

They have been identified through a meticulous examination of the seals and bottles. From there, a sequence of styles appeared. Collectors were then able to date the age of the bottle merely by its shape, if no seal were present.

While the English craftsmanship may have matched that of Italy, it was no secret that the material from which these pieces were made, were no match for that of those which were included in Venetian glass.

Ravenscroft and the London Glass-Sellers Co.

To try to rectify this, the London Glass-Sellers Company hired an expert by the name of George Ravenscroft to find a replacement for cristallo. Cristallo, by the way is totally clear glass.

His remedy? Ravenscroft added lead oxide -- in the form of litharge -- to the glass. This created an excellent material that not only equaled -- but exceeded -- the quality of Venetian glass.

Powdered flints were included in this new composition. Because of this, it was commonly called flint glass. Today, you'll hear it referred to as glass-of-lead.

Ravenscroft: First attempts unsuccessful

Don't think Ravenscroft met success on his first try. His initial pieces included a flaw called crisselling. This results in a fine crackle on the glass which clouds it.

By 1676, though, he appeared to have overcome this problem and he was granted permission to mark it in production with a seal of his choosing.

Appropriately, he chose a small seal with a raven's head in relief. You might not want to run out the door looking for this on glass now. It's said only about a dozen of these have actually survived. As you might expect, most of these are already safely locked away in museum.

Once glass-of-lead was perfected, craftsmen throughout Europe adopted it. It could not be blown as thinly as Venetian glass. But it was the perfect material for making items which were bright and colored compared with natural rock crystal.

Of 18th century glassware, the most popular was the production of wine glasses. Even today, thousands of glasses from that century survived. Of these, a myriad of patterns also exist.

Many of these had a "twist" stem. These glasses can be found in various colors, clear or in white. The earliest of these come with a folded foot, one in which the outer edge is turned under. The later ones possess just a plain, thin edge.

Politics affect craft of glassmaking

Economic politics, believe it or not, played a key role in the development of glass in the mid-1700s. England levied a duty -- or tax -- on all glass in 1745. Technically the duty amount was attached to the actual original material from which the glass was made.

So as a natural reaction, glassmakers just instinctively lessened the amount of these materials in each article in order to pay the smallest duty possible (makes total sense to me now!).

When this occurred, glassmakers compensated by putting more time and labor into the ornamentation of the articles. This, along with shifting fashion trends, accounts for the rise of the cutting, enameling and engraving of glass that eventually became so popular.

As the century progressed, three elements became even more important in glassware. The Beilby family of Newcastle on-Tyne, is famous for its work with enamel. By 1760, heavily cut decanters were introduced. It wasn't long after, that the principal decoration on most glasses was cutting.

Glass wasn't just for the manufacturer of wine glasses or decanters, though. In the last half of the 18th century, chandeliers and candelabras were popularized. These two items were in great demand, in fact. The complexity of the cut patterns glittered most brilliantly by candlelight.

And the hanging chains of small glass drops heightened this effect. You can still find a few original pieces if you search hard. Some, in fact, have even been converted for use with electricity.

Where did that come from? White glass from Bristol

Bristol, England soon became known for its porcelain-like white glass. Many times it was delicately painted in a fine array of colors. Originally, blue and amethyst-colored glass were the specialties of this town.

At Nailsea, which isn't far from Bristol, a good-size factory made jugs and rolling pins as well as other items for the kitchen. Many of these were manufactured out of green-tinted bottle glass. Because of this, they were taxed at a lower rate. In turn, this meant they could be sold cheaper than other glass items.

You'll hear collectors call these pieces simply "Nailsea" and "Bristol." But, wait, you probably realize by now that nothing is ever that simple in the antique world.

Yep, you guessed it. Similar pieces were soon being made throughout all of England. And yep! It's just about impossible to tell where a specific piece was actually made.

Let's talk some Irish, too!

No discussion of glassware would be complete without mentioning that crafted in Ireland.

And when you talk Ireland, there's only one name you need say: Waterford. Believe it or not, the antique collectors say, despite the stellar reputation, it's extremely difficult to tell Irish-made Waterford from English made examples during the same time period.

When the excise taxes were placed on English glass, more than one manufacturer sent craftsmen to Ireland to open factories there. Not much still remains from this period. Several identifiable pieces are just about all that are left at best and these are very few in number.

A few decanters, it's said, can still be found with verifiable inscriptions of Penrose, Waterford and Cork Glass. If you discover one labeled like this, you have a real find on your hands.

Now, that you have a short history of glassmaking in England, it's time to sail across the ocean to see what America was doing with glass at this time. The results may just surprise you! Or have you decided that nothing in antique collecting surprises you anymore?

CHAPTER 12- THE GREAT AMERICAN GLASSWARE QUEST

The year: 1609. The event: Captain John Smith of the New World sent a sample of glassware crafted in a fledgling colony. And that's about all that is really known with any certainty of the very early history of American glassware. Antique collectors and historians alike aren't even sure what type of piece was sent.

Disappointed? Many people are. It's speculated, just for the record, that the piece Capt. Smith sent was purely utilitarian. After all, 1609 was still very early in the settlement process. The colonists were still trying to survive in a new and often strange environment.

About the only needs the colonists really experienced for glass were bottles and window glass. And those two needs remained constant for a very long time.

The late 16th century saw attempts at establishing glasshouses. Richard Wistar, for example, advertised that in addition to nearly 400 boxes of window glass, he also sold lamp glass, bottles, snuff mustard receivers, as well as electrifying globes and tubes. (Hmm...sounds like an interesting assortment!)

Similarly, Henry William Steigel boasted in 1773 that among the items he sold were decanters, tumblers, wine glasses, jelly and cillabub glasses as well wide- mouth jars for sweetmeats and vials for doctors.

If you're searching for American glassware made prior to 1800, sadly, you'll find very little. Not surprisingly, it's because very little has actually survived. What is available, moreover, displays no single "American style." Rather, as might be expected, the styles depend on the native home of the craftsman who created them.

Among the two prominent styles were English and German. Immigrants from both of these countries worked in their native style (and what else would you expect?). This makes detecting anything you might call "genuinely American" nearly impossible.

Not only do you face this confusion, but the wares that came out of the several American glassmaking factories were nearly identical. (Oh, the search for authentic American glass is off to a fine start!)

Even if you could positively identify the particular piece as American-made, you'd be hard pressed to pinpoint where in the colonies it was made.

Interestingly, 18th century America experienced a great demand for pocket spirit flasks. (I guess that's one way to keep yourself warm during those frozen Valley Forge winters!) Demand was met by using a pleasantly ornamental mold.

The glassmakers blew the molten glass into the mold. The design of the mold then became impressed on the glass itself as it cooled. When the piece was completed cool and dried, the hand-mold would be opened and the completed flask removed.

Once the war for independence was won and the colonies were no longer under British domination, the government discouraged imports of any type of products. American manufacturing, at the same time, increased, including the number of glassworks.

But even with this, no single manufacturer could make a profit solely through the sale of table or ornamental wares. The mainstay of the vast majority of the businesses proved to be bottles and window glass.

Around the year 1828, a machine for the creation of pressed glassware was developed. This process involved the placement of molten glass into a mold, very similar to the process the earlier glassmakers did by hand.

Then a second mold was pressed on the glass while it was still molten, forcing it into shape.

Depending on the shape of the finished article, either one or both of the molds used may have ornamentation in them.

The method provided the quick -- and inexpensive -- creation of imitations of cut glass. Not only that, but it also allowed for the introduction of even more ornamentation than could have been performed on the wheel alone.

As you might expect, pressed colored glass appeared in large quantities, by a variety of glassware companies. Of these, though, probably none is more widely known than Boston and

Sandwich Glassworks, located in Sandwich, MA. It was founded in 1828 by Deming Jarves.

But similar, smaller operations were scattered throughout the country, which also created similar wares. And once again, the results are nearly the same as with pottery. It's difficult to distinguish what is made by the various glasswork factories.

To add to the confusion, the Boston and Sandwich firm also made fine paperweights nearly identical in style to those of the mid-19th century French variety which were so popular. Again, you can see how history has thrown a monkey wrench into your collector's plans. That's not to say you won't find pieces unique to this manufacturer, because you just may. It's not impossible.

Now, you also have a quick history of the glassware industry as well as seen from three very different perspectives. Still think antique hunting is in your future?

I sure hope you decide it is. These three categories only represent a small part of what collectors examine, read up on, and eventually buy. As you travel along your journey in antiquing, you'll have a better understanding of exactly what I mean.

CONCLUSION

You've Only Just Begun

This might be the portion of the book where we part company and go our separate ways, but I refuse to pronounce it "The End" of your interest in everything antique.

It's really just the beginning -- I hope -- of what will be a lifelong love affair with this indescribably satisfying hobby. I've barely been able to scratch the surface of what antiquing is all about.

But even then, you're now equipped with enough information on various antique items, prices, and buying tips that I'm confident you can venture forward in search of your Great American Antique.

Heck, for all I know, you might have already bought a piece of two while we were sailing through this book together. If so, good for you!

And if not, I can understand. You want to gaze at the Big Picture a while longer . . . linger with catalogs for a few further minutes . . . study the object just a moment or two more. And that's understandable.

After all, you're not just buying an object, you're investing in an antique. Everything about your purchase has to feel just right to you.

This is the one hobby you have that depends solely on your judgment as well as your feelings and opinions about whether a purchase or anything else about the hobby is right for you.

I can't tell you what price to pay for an antique or whether to invest in it at all. The decision is solely yours! And that's a good thing.

Hopefully, the pages of this book have provided you with some background to make an intelligent decision regarding that item you're thinking of purchasing.

The one thing I do wish for you is that this is a hobby that lasts a lifetime. It has all the earmarks for a wonderful, relaxing future . . . strolls through small towns . . . stops along the way into small, dusty antique shops . . . and plenty of friendly, knowledgeable folks to meet and to befriend.

Plus the wonderful finds of an era gone by.

What more could anyone ask of a hobby?

Happy Antiquing!

APPENDIX I: ENGLISH FURNITURE MAKERS AND DESIGNERS

The list is far too long to describe each and every furniture designers' specialty. Instead, I'm listing the most well-known English furniture makers. This gives you at least a familiarity with their names.

Additionally, I've listed the year of their births and deaths, when known. At the very least, when nothing else is known about their lives, I've listed the years they were crafting furniture. Armed with this information, you're well on your way to becoming a knowledgeable antique collector.

- **Samuel Bennett**
- **William Kent (1686-1748)**
- **John Cobb (d.1778)**
- **William Vile (d.1767)**
- **William Ince**
- **John Mayhew**
- **George Seddon (1729-1801)**
- **George Hepplewhite (d.1786)**
- **Gillow's**
- **Thomas Sheraton (1751-1806)**
- **William Moore (worked from 1780-1815)**

ABOUT THE AUTHOR

Hello, my name is Bowe Chaim Packer and I like to see myself as an open, *"wear my heart out on my sleeve"* kind of guy.

Some of the most important things to me in my life are:

- Laughing
- Kissing
- Holding hands
- Being playful
- Smiling
- Talking deeply with others
- Being loved
- Loving others
- Changing the world one person at a time (if my presence in your life doesn't make a difference then why am I here?) Hmmmmm, maybe that is a topic for another book. ;-)
- Learning from others (although often times I first resist). However, don't give up on me....
- Sharing ideas (no matter what they might be)
- Learning about others via most forms of contact.
- Traveling – hello, of course – almost forgot one of my favorite pass times.

Remember, LIFE is a journey for each and every one of us. We must never forget the things that are important to us or lose sight of what makes us happy.